From the
Olive Grove

From the Olive Grove

MEDITERRANEAN COOKING WITH OLIVE OIL

HELEN KOUTALIANOS & ANASTASIA KOUTALIANOS

ARSENAL
PULP PRESS

From the Olive Grove: Mediterranean Cooking with Olive Oil

Copyright © 2010 by Helen and Anastasia Koutalianos

ARSENAL PULP PRESS
#101-211 East Georgia St.
Vancouver, BC
Canada V6A 1Z6
arsenalpulp.com

The publisher gratefully acknowledges the support of the Government of Canada through the Book Publishing Industry Development Program and the Government of British Columbia through the Book Publishing Tax Credit Program for its publishing activities.

The author and publisher assert that the information contained in this book is true and complete to the best of their knowledge. All recommendations are made without guarantee on the part of the author and Arsenal Pulp Press. The author and publisher disclaim any liability in connection with the use of this information. For more information, contact the publisher.

Photography by Darla Furlani
Book Design by Electra Design Group

Printed and bound in Hong Kong

Library and Archives Canada Cataloguing in Publication

Koutalianos, Helen, 1950-
    From the olive grove : Mediterranean cooking with olive oil / Helen & Anastasia Koutalianos.

Includes index.
Issued also in an electronic format.
ISBN 978-1-55152-367-5

    1. Cookery (Olive oil). 2. Olive oil. 3. Cookery, Mediterranean.
I. Koutalianos, Anastasia, 1980- II. Title.

TX819.O42K68 2010   641.6'463   C2010-902973-9

To Basil, Vicki, Anastasia, and Evangeline: the reasons for all my cooking.

With love,
Mom

CONTENTS

PREFACE

Our single-estate family olive grove is in the west Peloponnese region of Greece. The hilly landscape, about twelve miles (nineteen km) from the sea, is peppered with relics of the past. The panoramic views are breathtaking and the region's natural beauty is unmatched; fruit, olive, pine, and cypress trees line the slopes, with vegetable farms and vineyards nestled in-between. Here we grow Koroneiki olives and Corinthian currant grapes, which we use to produce our award-winning extra virgin olive oil and balsamic vinegar.

For four generations, our family has been producing olive oil. Our olive grove is certified organic, which means we don't use chemical fertilizers or sprays; our farming practices are similar to those of our fathers, grand-fathers, and great-grand-fathers. (Some consumers believe that organic foods are too expensive, but there are enormous "hidden" costs to foods that have been grown with pesticides, which affect our health and the environment. And with increasing consumer demands, organic foods are becoming more affordable and accessible.)

Basil, my husband, takes enormous pride in harvesting the olives we grow. Each October, he makes his annual trek from Vancouver to Greece, where he spends the next two-and-a-half months. His time there takes great patience and endurance, as we strive for high standards in the production of our olive oil. He is often challenged by bad weather (too much rain, or not enough) and a tight timeline in which to assemble a work crew, organize the harvest, oversee the olive press, and prepare our oil for shipment. None of this could be done without our family and friends in Greece, who help us to maintain the grove and produce the oil.

For years, we gave bottles of our olive oil as gifts to friends. Everyone loved it and always asked for more. In 1997, Basil and I decided to bring our olive oil to Canada. We have been privileged to introduce our extra virgin olive oil to food lovers and feel blessed to do something we truly love.

The cuisine offered in this book is inspired by the olive oil we grow and produce. It includes a blend of modern fare, creations by renowned chefs Basil and I have met over the years, and treasured Greek and Mediterranean family recipes, passed down from generation to generation. When I was growing up, all of our meals were made from scratch—there was no fast food. You cannot rush perfection. I remember the mouth-watering aromas from slow-cooked foods that would greet us at the door when we got home. My mother (Evangeline) and grandmother (Anastasia) were both great cooks. I loved cooking with my grandmother, who encouraged my participation in the kitchen and was a perfectionist, especially when it came to making dolmades (stuffed grape leaves). This recipe (p. 155) calls for quality olive oil, and a lot of it! My mother and grandmother taught me how to make everything from bread (p. 164) to quail with olives (which to this day is my favorite—you can find the recipe on p. 110). I owe my talents in the kitchen to them.

In writing this cookbook, I want to share with readers the true versatility of olive oil, beyond its better known uses in Greek cuisine. Olive oil is flavorful, and not just for drizzling on salads; it's a healthy oil that can be used to sauté or fry foods, make delicious cakes and cookies, and even as an ingredient in ice cream (p. 185; 187). In Greece and throughout the Mediterranean, we use olive oil liberally, as part of a well-balanced diet containing a moderate amount of meat, plenty of seafood, and fresh fruit and vegetables. Olive oil is some-times called "liquid sunshine"; it is real food, that is, it has life and vitality, and isn't riddled with chemical additives. It is also a functional food, helping to prevent disease and increase health and well-being.

When I taught Greek cooking classes, the students always told me how wonderful everything tasted. The lesson was that fresh herbs, proper seasoning, the use of local and organic produce, and good quality olive oil enhance the taste of food. As producers of olive oil, we have filled these pages with tips on how to choose a great olive oil and how to use it in healthy meals your dinner guests and family will enjoy. Eat well. And as the Greeks say, *kali orexi* (bon appétit)!
—*Helen Koutalianos*

PREFACE

I've always loved the kitchen, and more importantly, food. I remember being ten or eleven years old and getting to stay home on a school day because I didn't feel well. I would end up in the kitchen pretending to be a cooking show host. I was Julia Child, voice and all, and created imaginary but magnificent meals for hours. When I was a kid, I loved to help my mom stir whatever she was making. Anything that needed stirring, I was there. Even to this day, sure, I'll cut the veggies if you need me to, but stirring—you don't have to ask—I'm already on it!

The first thing my mom asks when we talk on the phone is, "What did you eat today?" Food has always been a big thing in my family. Our kitchen and pantry were filled with great olive oil, hand-picked dried spices, grains and roasted nuts, and homemade preserves, sauces, and wine. Every summer since I can remember, my parents have been going to the Okanagan in southern British Columbia to pick ripe tomatoes so we could can our own sauce. We chopped and blended each tomato and boiled the sauce in a huge cauldron over the old backyard sandbox. Over 200 pounds of tomatoes each time!

Good food was a constant in my family's home and still is. My mother made us home-cooked meals every night. The kitchen was packed with fruit, fresh fish, game meat (my dad loves to fish and hunt), herbs, veggies from the garden—and an abundance of love. My father would always say of me, "This kid, she knows how to eat." I would make weird culinary concoctions, adding Dijon mustard, splashes of olive oil, and spices to any meal; I've always been creative in the kitchen! I'm also the child who, on a trip to Greece at the age of ten, fell asleep with her head in the plate of tzatziki.

To this day, our whole family gravitates toward the kitchen whenever my mom is cooking. It's our place to share and create, and my mom is a great teacher. She is patient and cooks with love. And she is a storyteller—a gift she's passed on to me.

In 2007 I went back to school to study magazine and book publishing. It was then that I got the idea to write a cookbook filled with my mother's recipes. At the time, my parents' company, Basil Olive Oil Products, was entering its tenth year of business, and I figured this would be a great way to celebrate all their hard work. I rifled through her recipe binders and newspaper clippings from the food column she'd written for a local newspaper—and there were a lot—and through cookbooks full of hand-written scribbles and food-stained pages. Soon we had some 200 recipes ready to go.

The dishes were predominantly Greek and Mediterranean, and while olive oil is often associated with these cuisines, we didn't want to limit the recipes to one geographic area. We decided to approach some of the chefs who use our olive oil to see if they would like to contribute recipes to our cookbook. And sure enough, they were excited to be involved. The chefs come from all parts of the world and contributed recipes reflecting a range of cuisines, including West Coast, French, and contemporary.

Testing all the recipes turned into an interesting process. Our kitchen became a science lab as we precisely measured our ingredients and tasted, tasted, tasted our dishes. This was actually the best part: I got to stir my heart out!

Some years ago, my mother and I talked about what we'd leave to our families when we passed. She said she'd leave her family recipes. At first I didn't understand; what kind of legacy is that? Aren't legacies supposed to be larger than life? Now I get it. These recipes have been such a vital part of our lives. And this cookbook is a celebration of our family to share with all families.

—Anastasia (Stasia) Koutalianos

ACKNOWLEDGMENTS

This cookbook was a labor of love, and its success is shared by an inspiring team of food lovers.

To my mother Evangeline and grandmother Anastasia, thank you for teaching me not to be afraid in the kitchen and to be inventive in the way I prepare food for my family. Through this cookbook, your legacy lives on.

To Basil, thank you for all your hard work. We did it! To Vicki, I hope these recipes nourish your family as they have mine. Your clever pitch sealed the deal. The world is your oyster. To my daughter Anastasia, for writing the cookbook proposal and never giving up; thank you, child. I couldn't have done it without you. To Dr Evangeline, your future is full and bright. For your informative bit on the health benefits of olive oil, thank you, dear.

To our photographer, Darla Furlani, your creativity speaks volumes! Thanks to the wonderful chefs who contributed unique and tasty recipes: Christophe Kwiatkowsky, David Beston, Frank Pabst, Jean-Francis Quaglia, Liana Robberecht, Lisa Ahier, Lynda Larouche, Robert Clark, Robert Cordonier, Ronald St Pierre, Tony Minichiello, James Walt, and Vincent Stufano. Thanks to Whole Foods Market for supplying the fresh organic produce for our photo shoot. And to the wonderful staff at Arsenal Pulp Press, without whom this cookbook would not be possible, thank you for your hard work and for believing in real food.

—Helen Koutalianos

INTRODUCTION

A Brief History of Olive Oil

The olive tree was first cultivated around 6,000 BCE, and yet historians are still baffled by the plant's origins. Artifacts discovered at archaeological sites suggest that the practice of olive oil cultivation began in central Persia and later spread to Greece, the Mediterranean basin, and northern Africa. To this day, ninety percent of olives are grown in this region.

Olive oil was once the most highly traded commodity in the ancient world and the olive tree played a role in many ancient civilizations. In Egypt, olive oil was used for cooking, medicine, and religious purposes, such as anointing the dead and to light lanterns for rituals. In Greece, the olive tree was revered as sacred and seen as a symbol of respect. The tree was praised for its food and medicinal properties. Excavations reveal the culture's sophisticated techniques for storage and extraction of oil. By the sixth century CE, the Greeks had become major exporters of oil throughout the Mediterranean. The Romans spread the fruit of the olive tree throughout their empire. They cured olives and mastered the method of oil extraction, inventing the screw press, perfecting the storage and distribution of olive oil, and making its sale a lucrative business. Imperial taxes were paid to Rome in bulk oil. But the fall of the Roman Empire caused a reduction in the scale of olive production. By the end of the Middle Ages, however, the cultivation of olives had expanded once again, due in part to improved transportation and trade between northern and southern Europe. And from the Christian church's earliest days, olive oil illuminated its halls, embalmed its dead, and was used to bless its religious figures.

For centuries, the production of olives and olive oil was managed by small estate, family businesses. But the nineteenth century saw the development of industrial oil-refining plants and large-scale growing and production cooperatives. Small amounts of olive oil remained in each producing country, while vast amounts of olives went to central refineries to be made into amalgamated oil blends that were then marketed worldwide.

By the 1970s, consumers were intrigued by the nutritional benefits of the Mediterranean diet and olive oil. Many wished to move beyond the widely available, cheap tinned olive oils that weren't of the best quality and began to seek out high-quality oils produced on a small scale.

Today the olive tree is cultivated worldwide and is found in countries including the US, Mexico, several South American countries, China, and South Africa. Its global expansion is a true testament to the growing demand for olive oil.

THE OLIVE TREE

The olive tree is an evergreen, with leaves that are dark green on one side and a lighter silvery color on the other. It tends to grow between thirty and forty degrees latitude and in elevations up to 1,300 feet (400 meters) high. Some trees require very fertile soil, while others can grow well on rocky hillsides. To produce abundant fruit, olive trees like well-drained soil and prefer alkaline conditions, although they can tolerate most acidic soils. The tree thrives in hot dry summers and mild, moist, and temperate winters—more or less a Mediterranean climate. As such, the olive tree can withstand high heat and drought but cannot tolerate prolonged humidity in the summertime. The olive tree is also sensitive to cold (below 32°F/0°C), and its leaves are susceptible to mold, especially during the growing period, but it requires cooler temperatures in the winter to induce a dormant state so the tree can rest. Cool winters induce flowers to bud, but harsh winters will wither the fruit and cause it to fall or prevent flowers from budding altogether.

We generally irrigate our trees two to three times during the sweltering summer months, being careful not to over-water (which would increase the olives' water content, making them less flavorful and aromatic). If the olives don't get enough water, on the other hand, they'll end up looking like raisins.

There are hundreds of olive varieties grown worldwide, each with its own distinct characteristics, including the Koroneiki, which we grow in Greece, the Manzanilla de Jaén in Spain, and the Frantoio in Italy. Some are grown for table olives, others for olive oil production. Most varieties are self-pollinating, but in order for a wild olive seed to first germinate, it must pass through the digestive system of a bird.

The olive tree is a biennial crop: a big olive harvest one year is followed by a small one the next, with another bumper crop in year three. A small yield puts great economic strain on the farmer, but also gives relief to the laborers. If the olive tree were to produce fruitful crops every year, it would be difficult to pick the olives in time. Regular pruning, irrigation, and fertilizing will counteract the tree's natural tendency to biennial cropping and ensure a steady yield.

The olive tree produces many tiny white flowers in late spring. By summer, these have developed into olives, although only a small fraction of the flowers become fruit. The tree naturally sheds its surplus fruit before it fully matures, so that it isn't burdened by more olives than it can support. An olive tree takes four to five years to yield its first fruit, and ten to fifteen years to reach its full fruit-bearing capacity.

The unripe olive is pear-shaped and green in color. It changes from green to purple and lastly to black when fully mature. The olive fruit is fully ripe (black) six months after the flower has blossomed, but the best oil is produced from the fruit while it is young (green). Olives pressed for oil can be picked at any stage; however, the more unripe the olive, the less oil it will yield. Picking olives while they're still green is referred to as the early harvest.

The olive tree should be pruned every year, and this is done either by hand or mechanically. Pruning structures the tree by balancing out the branches and making them equal in size. By exposing the fruit to the sun and distributing energy to the tree's new shoots, pruning increases the number of fruit-bearing growths and therefore the productivity of the trees. We do "rough" pruning—cutting branches loaded with olives and leaving the less burdened branches to grow bigger next year—in October and November, during the harvest period; then in February and March we prune before the olives flower ("fine" pruning). Mature trees are usually fertilized every three years, near the end of winter, again at the end of spring—when the olive tree has flowered—or at the end of the summer, when it rains.

Fertilizing, like pruning, can help counter the olive tree's biennial cropping. The tree grows best when watered, pruned, and fertilized, and these all help increase the yield of olives.

The olive tree is subject to a variety of pests and diseases, but the olive fruit fly (*Bactrocera oleae*) is the tree's worst enemy. An iridescent fly, it bites into the olive and lays an egg in the developing fruit, and there the larva will feed on the pulp. Infected olives usually drop to the ground, but if harvested and pressed, the larva will give the olive oil a "dirty" taste. To combat the prevalence of disease, trees are either sprayed with chemicals or have sulfur traps hanging on their branches (an organic method). Spraying the leaves against the olive fly will prevent damage to the tree and its fruit, but the chemicals will also be absorbed by the plant.

HARVESTING

The art of making great olive oil begins with the harvest. During the harvest, the fruits can be easily bruised or damaged, which will accelerate the oxidation process and produce an unpleasant-tasting, lower quality oil. When picked, the olives need to be healthy, with no blemishes and free from pests and disease. A cut in the olive's skin can lead to bacterial infection, yeast, or fungi, which can also ruin the oil.

There are several ways to pick olives. Handpicking is the most laborious and time-consuming, but ensures the best quality oil. Pickers climb ladders and comb the olives with wooden rakes. Tarps are slung in the trees and stretched just above the ground to catch the olives as they fall to prevent them from bruising and to avoid any contact with the soil, which may stick to the olives and leave an unwanted taste.

The collection of our Koroneiki olives is done in the early part of the harvest season (November). Picking olives early ensures our oil is low in acidity (making it extra virgin) and high in nutritional value. Basil and the workers first place tarps under each tree to collect the olives and make sure the fruit doesn't come into contact with the soil. In years past, the harvest was a time when families worked together to pick and press the olives. Today, our family is dispersed, so we rely on work crews. The harvest is very labor-intensive and begins with the picking of the olives while they are still green. Green olives have the highest nutritional value but produce less oil—a fair trade-off in our eyes. The workers pile the collected olives into burlap sacks and send them to the olive mill for the first cold pressing.

Pickers can also strike the olive branches to rattle the olives and allow them to drop into the nets. This method may take less time, but it can also bruise the fruit and damage the tree, leaving the olives susceptible to disease and increased oxidation, especially if left in the heat. For larger groves, machines are used to shake the trees and rattle the olives free. This works well for big cooperatives, but can also damage the fruit and tree branches.

The longer the fruit remains on the tree, the more oil will be produced upon extraction, but most producers tend to pick their olives while they are still green, which ensures the freshest olive oil. Younger olives are also high in polyphenols and low in linoleic acid, both of which help delay the oxidation, decay, and rancidity of the fruit.

PRESSING AND PROCESSING

The pressing of olives is a relatively simple process. It takes about ten pounds (4.5 kg) of olives to produce one quart/liter of olive oil. The best olive oil producers press within twenty-four hours after the harvest to minimize damage to the fruit and ensure a quality oil. Olives left in the heat are subject to oxidation, which will increase the oil's acidity. (An olive's oil acidity level is the true measure of its quality and can only be determined by chemical analysis.) There are three main methods of pressing—millstone, sinolea, and mechanical press. Deciding which pressing method to use is crucial; it will impact the amount and quality of oil produced.

With millstone pressing, two or three millstones are used to crush the washed fruit and pits into a paste so the fruit starts to excrete oil. Millstone presses extract up to forty percent of the oil from the first press. Traditionally, the paste is spread evenly over small, round woven-rope mats, piled thirty or forty mats high and stacked between metal discs. These are then placed in a hydraulic press. The mats are designed to allow the liquid to trickle down the stack and collect at the bottom in stainless steel vats. The reddish-brown liquid is part oil and part natural olive vegetable water. To separate the oil and water, the liquid is either placed in a centrifuge or is left alone so the oil floats to the top on its own. The centrifuge spins the olive paste at high speeds to separate the mixture of oil, water, and olive solids. Hot water is sometimes added to the remaining olive paste to produce the second pressing, resulting in a hot-pressed oil (a designation never found on a label). The oil is skimmed off and stored in underground tanks or in stainless steel barrels. Olive oil will appear cloudy until the sediment has settled, which can take up to a few months.

A newer method, popular in Italy, is the use of the sinolea machine. After the olives are crushed, the olive paste goes into the sinolea, a large tank with thousands of vibrating stainless steel blades. The machine uses vibrations to allow the oil to float to the top of the paste where it is skimmed off. This process releases only thirty percent of the oil but uses almost no heat; while it is expen-sive, it produces top quality olive oil.

Modern mechanical presses, such as the ones we use, can extract up to ninety percent of the oil from the fruit. The collected fruit arrives at the mill where the olives are washed and the leaves and twigs removed. Once washed, the olives are crushed, pits and all; this breaks open the olive's skin. The olive mash passes through a malixer (a large vat with a spiral blade). Warm (but not hot!) water in the walls of the vat helps to extract the oil. Then the mash goes through a process known as "centrifugation," in which the pulp is separated from the water. At this point, the olives are pressed for the first time ("first press") while a decanter sepa-rates the oil from the fruit mash. Basil checks the temperature to ensure it is below 86°F (30°C)—that is, it is "cold-pressed." At this point, we begin to enjoy the aroma of the fresh green (or *agourelaio*) oil. And we get to have our first taste! With bread in hand, we sample the first press of the new harvest. Our Golden Olive "Eleni" oil is then placed in barrels and shipped to Vancouver. There, we bottle and distribute it to local markets, restaurants, and all olive oil lovers.

SINGLE ESTATE AND BLENDED OILS

Olive oil is either bottled and distributed as single estate oil, such as ours, or is sold to industrial plants to be processed and often blended into olive oil of various grades. In recent years, single estate producers have gained a reputation for stocking shelves with high quality oils, and their products therefore come with a higher price tag. Organic olive oils are equally as expensive, and rightfully so, for organic farmers incur higher costs in cultivation, harvesting methods, and soil management than conventional farmers. While commercially made extra virgin olive oils are purchased in bulk, blended to a particular taste, and sold cheaply, the quality of these oils is questionable. It is common practice that olive oil-producing countries, when in need, buy from neighboring producers and blend the oils for sale abroad, so it isn't possible to determine an oil's country of origin. Mass-produced oils, typically blends of refined oils splashed with higher grades to add a hint of flavor and aroma, are often disguised as first-press, high quality oils, but these products are priced too low to be superior oils. Supermarket brands are also typically not the freshest; they remain on the store shelves for months on end, are exposed to fluorescent lights (leading to more oxidation), and seldom indicate when the oil was harvested and pressed. Olive oil should be consumed within one to two years from its date of harvest. To purchase the freshest oil, look for labels that indicate the oil's date of harvest, acidity level, certifying bodies (if purchasing organic), and whether the olive oil is cold-pressed extra virgin, and first press.

And if your market offers olive oil taste tests, be sure to taste before buying.

OLIVE OIL GRADES AND PROCESSING TERMS

An olive oil's quality and taste is affected by many factors, including the variety of olive, the olive farm's soil management, irrigation, and pruning practices, the climate and altitude at which the olives were grown, the health and ripeness of the fruit when picked, and the harvest and extraction methods. Many people think the quality of an olive oil can be determined by its taste, color, and aroma, but in order to truly test for nutritional qualities, the oil must undergo a chemical analysis that measures its fat content and acidity levels. Olive oils vary in taste from sweet and mild to grassy and peppery. There are excellent oils in all flavors, aromas, and colors, regardless of the producing country. Here are some points to keep in mind when buying olive oil:

Acidity is the measure of an oil's fatty acid content and an indicator of its quality. Good quality oils will proudly showcase their acidity levels on their product labels.

Cold press means temperatures during the pressing of the olives have not exceeded 82–86°F (28–30°C).

The **color** of an oil ranges from pale yellow to intense green; however, it is not an indicator of quality. Rather, color is an indicator of the olive variety and/or the olive's maturity when picked. At the same time, not all green olive oil is necessarily made from olives that were green when picked.

Date of harvest tells us when the olives were picked and pressed. Rarely is this information included on the label, but it does give buyers an idea of how fresh the oil is. Unlike wine, olive oil loses its nutritional value, aroma, and flavor as time goes on. It is best to consume your oil within one to two years of its date of harvest, when the oil is at its best.

Extra light olive oil is an American term that suggests fewer calories but actually denotes an oil that has been refined and blended with other oils to give it a light color and taste.

Extra virgin olive oil is the highest quality olive oil grade, with an acidity content of 0.8 percent or less (according to International Olive Oil Council standards). This oil offers the best quality, aroma, flavor, and color, though not all extra virgin olive oils taste and look the same. Extra virgin olive oils with acidity levels under 0.5 percent are high in antioxidants and have greater resistance to rancidity.

First press is the olive oil produced after the olives have been pressed only once. Note that not all first-press oils are necessarily also cold-pressed.

Lampante (or virgin lampante) olive oil is high in acidity (three percent and above), has undergone chemical refining, and may be blended with virgin olive oils to give it flavor and aroma, but it is not considered food-grade oil on its own. It may be included in oil blends sold as "pure," "refined," or even "extra light."

Olive oil is a blend of refined and virgin olive oils. Refined oil has no taste or smell, so virgin olive oil is added to it to give it flavor. The taste, smell, and acidity of an olive oil blend vary with the amount of virgin olive oil added.

Olive pomace oil is chemically extracted from the olive mash (made up of pits and olive skins) left on the woven mats during millstone pressing. In the past, this paste was typically fed to pigs in Greece. Nowadays, oil can be extracted from the pomace using chemicals and heat, then refined with more high heat. Pomace oil is sold cheaply to restaurants for use in frying. It is also used in treating wool, making soaps, and manufacturing toiletries. Pomace oil can also be flavored with other grades of olive oil and sold.

Refined olive oil has been chemically cleaned to eradicate high acidity, oxidation, or any unpleasant taste. Refined oil is sometimes made from lampante oil.

Virgin olive oil is a good quality olive oil, with an acidity level ranging from 0.8 percent to 2.5 percent. It has adequate aroma, flavor, and color to use in cooking, but is not as choice as an extra virgin olive oil. Due to its higher acidity level, virgin olive oil may go rancid more quickly than extra virgin olive oils; as such, it has a shorter shelf life.

HEALTH

Olive oil is essential to Greek cuisine (in fact, Greeks consume more olive oil per capita than any other nationality!). Mediterranean diets, rich in olive oil, grains, fish, and fresh fruit and vegetables, are known to lower the risk of heart disease, colon and breast cancers, and diabetes, and to be rich in health-promoting essential fatty acids, vitamins and minerals, and antioxidants.

Health experts agree that the type of fat we consume has a bearing on our health. In order to understand why the types of fats found in olive oil are good for our health, we need to understand what makes some fats good for us and others unhealthy. There are three types of dietary fat: saturated, mono-unsaturated, and poly-unsaturated.

WHEN BUYING OLIVE OIL ...

Look for these terms on the label:

- cold-pressed
- date of harvest and best-before date
- extra virgin
- first press
- low acidity levels
- single-estate origin
- accredited certification logos (if purchasing certified organic olive oils)

AVOID:

- refined or blended olive oil
- pure, light, or lampante (or virgin lampante) olive oil
- cheap oils claiming to be extra virgin, first press, or cold-pressed

Saturated fats are often (but not always) of animal origin, while mono-unsaturated and poly-unsaturated fats are derived mainly from plants. Olive oil is high in mono- and poly-unsaturated fats—both of which have many health benefits—in fact, it is comprised of seventy percent mono-unsaturated, twenty to twenty-five percent poly-unsaturated, and five to ten percent saturated fats.

Fats are defined by the chemical bonds between carbon atoms. Saturated fats have single bonds between carbon atoms, while unsaturated fats (both mono- and poly-) have a double carbon bond. Mono-unsaturated fats are healthier for us because of this structure. Their carbon double bond creates a kink in the chain of carbons, making it harder for multiple mono-unsaturated fatty acids to bind to one another. Think of it this way: sheets of paper are easiest to layer on top of one another when they are smooth, straight, and flat; crumpled-up paper is difficult to stack and will leave gaps between each sheet. Unsaturated fatty chains—like those found in olive oil—are like the crumpled paper: their structure prevents fatty plaque from building up on the arteries.

Our bodies cannot produce essential oleic acid (a mono-unsaturated fat) or omega-3 and omega-6 fatty acids (both poly-unsaturated). These essential fatty acids (EFAs) are needed to insulate cells and provide our bodies with a healthy, slowly released energy source. Omega-3 essential fatty acids—found in olive oil—also tend to have an anti-inflammatory effect on the arteries, helping to remove clots and allow for an efficient circulatory system.

Cholesterol is a major component of every cell in the body, especially the brain and nervous system. There is both "bad" and "good" cholesterol, however. Bad cholesterol, or low density lipoprotein (LDL), transports and deposits fat and cholesterol in the blood vessels and tissues, and levels of LDL increase with a high intake of saturated fats. A diet high in saturated fats also increases the risk of high blood pressure, heart attacks, and strokes. But good cholesterol, that is, high density lipoprotein or HDL, removes free cholesterol from the blood vessels and carries it to the liver, where it is eliminated. The high mono-unsaturated fat content of olive oil decreases our LDL levels (and other fats in the blood) without diminishing our good cholesterol. And high quality olive oil is also high in antioxidants (containing thirty to forty antioxidant compounds)—higher than most seed oils (e.g., canola, sunflower, safflower, etc.).

Antioxidants are substances that slow down and neutralize oxidation in the cells and the formation of cell-damaging free radicals—which are linked to diseases such as cancer. The antioxidants in olive oil also contribute to lowering both systolic and diastolic blood pressure. Antioxidants such as vitamin E (found in olive oil) are known to reduce the incidence of atherosclerosis, increase the efficiency of the circulatory system and immune function, and may play a role in slowing the aging process.

These health benefits provide many compelling reasons to enjoy a diet rich in olive oil. The delicious, nutritious, and easy-to-prepare recipes that follow show you just how to add more health-boosting olive oil to every meal.

HEALTH BENEFITS ATTRIBUTED TO THE CONSUMPTION OF OLIVE OIL:

- helps the absorption of calcium and may play a role in the prevention of osteoporosis
- inhibits inflammation
- as a mono-unsaturated fat, protects the brain against cognitive decline and dementia
- aids in digestion
- is a diuretic
- reduces gastric acidity and helps protect against ulcers
- may help lower the risk of colon cancer
- prevents constipation, stimulates bile secretion, and lowers the risk of gallstones
- protects the body's mucous membranes and stimulates the gallbladder

- provides vital essential fatty acids for the development of an unborn baby's bones, brain, and nervous system
- reduces the effect of aging on the skin, organs, and brain (some studies have shown that there is a low incidence of skin cancer among Mediterranean populations, and olive oil seems to be a contributing factor: it contains significantly higher amounts of the anticancer agent squalene than seed oils)
- speeds the healing of cuts
- may play a role in lowering risk of breast cancer, thanks to its polyphenol antioxidant content
- helps lower blood pressure

OLIVE OIL ENERGY DRINK

Vital veggies and EFA-rich olive oil make for a drink that will give you energy throughout the day.

1 cup fresh spinach
1 small cucumber
¼ cup parsley
1 stalk celery
1 cup water

sea salt, to taste
3-4 tbsp olive oil
dash of cayenne pepper
juice of ½ a lemon

Combine all ingredients in a blender or food processor and blend well.
Drink immediately.

BASIL PESTO

GARLIC AIOLI

HUMMUS (Chickpea Dip)

TIROKAFTERI (Pepper & Feta Dip)

TZATZIKI (Yogurt & Cucumber Dip)

KALAMATA OLIVE TAPENADE

PARMESAN CHEESE DIP

MELITZANOSALATA (Eggplant Dip)

TARAMOSALATA (Fish Roe Spread)

BALSAMIC FIG BRUSCHETTA WITH BLUE CHEESE FILLING

FETA CHEESE-STUFFED HOT BANANA PEPPERS

— *Appetizers* —

THREE EASY ACCOMPANIMENTS TO KEBABS

GRILLED VEGETABLES

ARTICHOKES WITH DILL MUSTARD SAUCE

MELITZANOKEFTEDES (Eggplant Balls)

ROASTED RED BELL PEPPERS

FETA WITH HONEY-ROSEMARY OLIVE OIL DRESSING

SAGANAKI (Fried Cheese)

ESCARGOT IN TOMATO-WINE SAUCE

ESCARGOT WITH ROSEMARY

OYSTERS CAPARI

TARAMOKEFTEDES (Fish Roe Rissoles)

SMELTS IN WHITE WINE WITH SAVORY SAVORO SAUCE

AVOCADO CRAB CAKES

BASIL PESTO

Rub this pesto onto chicken (whole or pieces) before baking or serve over pasta of choice. Pour any leftover sauce into an ice-cube tray and freeze. Once frozen, place pesto cubes in a plastic freezer bag and use a few cubes at a time to flavor soups or pasta sauces as needed.

1½ cups fresh basil
4 garlic cloves
½ cup pine nuts
3 tbsp grated Parmesan cheese
1 tsp lemon juice
½ cup olive oil
sea salt, to taste

In a food processor on medium speed, blend the basil, garlic, pine nuts, cheese, and lemon juice. Reduce the speed to low and slowly drizzle in the olive oil, until the mixture emulsifies. Add salt to taste.

Makes about 1 cup.

GARLIC AIOLI

A tangy dip for any occasion. Serve with crab cakes or pan-fried fish, or as a dip for calamari (squid) (p. 135).

2 egg yolks*, at room temperature
4–6 garlic cloves, crushed
1 tsp Dijon mustard (optional)
½ tsp sea salt
freshly ground black pepper, to taste
1–2 tsp lemon juice
¾ cup olive oil

*If desired, first partially coddle the egg yolks: Add whole, unbeaten yolks to a metal bowl and place over simmering water (like a bain-marie or double boiler) for about a minute, making sure they don't begin to solidify. (The point isn't to cook the egg but to get rid of any bacteria.) Remove from heat.

In a food processor, add egg yolks, garlic, mustard, salt, pepper, and lemon juice. Mix well, making sure garlic is puréed. With the processor set on low speed, slowly drizzle in the olive oil. Continue to blend until mixture is thick and has emulsified. Refrigerate until served.

Makes 1 cup.

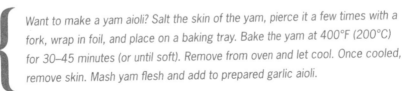

Want to make a yam aioli? Salt the skin of the yam, pierce it a few times with a fork, wrap in foil, and place on a baking tray. Bake the yam at 400°F (200°C) for 30–45 minutes (or until soft). Remove from oven and let cool. Once cooled, remove skin. Mash yam flesh and add to prepared garlic aioli.

HUMMUS (Chickpea Dip)

Chickpeas (garbanzo beans) and Greek cuisine go hand-in-hand. Hummus is a great spread for crackers, corn chips, pita bread, and sandwiches. For a more subtle flavor, roast the garlic first.

2 cups cooked chickpeas (or 1 17-oz/500-mL can)
⅓ cup sesame seeds or tahini, a ground sesame paste
4–6 garlic cloves, crushed
juice of 1 lemon
½ cup olive oil
¼ cup finely chopped fresh parsley
1 tsp sea salt
½ tsp powdered coriander seed (optional)

In a food processor, combine all ingredients and blend until smooth. Chill before serving.

Makes 2 cups.

TIROKAFTERI (Pepper & Feta Dip)

One of my husband Basil's favorite dishes; it's a little bit spicy (depending on how hot the banana pepper is) yet tamed by the rich and creamy cheese filling. Serve as an appetizer with bread or crackers, or, as the Greeks do, have it with your breakfast. For extra flavor, blend a peeled and seeded tomato into the cheese filling.

1 hot banana pepper, grilled
1 tbsp olive oil
1 cup crumbled goat feta cheese
½ cup olive oil

Set oven to broil.

Remove top of banana pepper, core and seed it, then cut lengthwise into slices. Place on a baking sheet and brush with olive oil. Broil on each side until skin is lightly browned (about 2–5 minutes). Remove skin from pepper and discard.

In a food processor, combine the peppers, feta cheese, and olive oil. Blend until a smooth but thick texture is obtained. Refrigerate until ready to serve.

Makes 1½ cups.

TZATZIKI (Yogurt & Cucumber Dip)

The secret to great tzatziki is using high-fat yogurt and straining all the water from both the yogurt and the grated cucumber. Skimp on this process, and you'll end up with a watery dip, and then, trust me, the gods won't be happy! The best tzatziki is made ahead of time—this allows for a stronger garlic flavor. Make it the day before and refrigerate.

1 English cucumber
½ tsp sea salt
2 cups (500 mL) plain yogurt (5–10 percent milk fat)
2 garlic cloves, finely crushed
2 tbsp olive oil
1 tbsp white vinegar
sea salt, to taste

Equipment needed: cheesecloth

Grate the cucumber into a mixing bowl and mix in the salt. Place grated cucumber on a piece of cheesecloth stretched over a bowl and refrigerate overnight (or for at least 3–4 hours).

Place the yogurt onto a piece of cheesecloth stretched over a bowl and, as with the cucumber, allow it to drain for several hours or overnight.

Combine the strained yogurt and cucumber in a bowl, and add the garlic, olive oil, and vinegar. Blend well. Add more salt if needed. Refrigerate until ready to serve.

Makes 2–2½ cups.

KALAMATA OLIVE TAPENADE

Greeks love their Kalamata olives. This spread showcases the salty, rich flavor of the olive. Great on crackers, pizza, and in sandwiches.

1 cup Kalamata olives, rinsed and pitted
2 tbsp capers
1 garlic clove
1 cup pine nuts (optional)
3–4 whole anchovies (optional)
1 tbsp olive oil
1 tbsp lemon juice
½ tsp dried thyme or basil
½ tsp freshly ground black pepper
1½–2 cups chopped fresh parsley

Combine all ingredients in a food processor and purée until tapenade is smooth enough to spread.

Makes about 3 cups.

PARMESAN CHEESE DIP

For a sweeter flavor, roast the garlic cloves first. Dip in chunks of crusty French bread, and serve with Kalamata olives and icy-cold glasses of Retsina (a Greek white wine).

¼ cup olive oil
2–3 garlic cloves, finely minced
balsamic vinegar, to taste
1–2 tbsp grated Parmesan cheese

Combine all ingredients in a bowl and mix well.

Serve at room temperature.

Makes about ½ cup.

MELITZANOSALATA (Eggplant Dip)

Eggplants are a Greek's best friend. Roasted eggplants, even better! Melitzano-salata is served at most Greek tavernas and is delicious as a side, or on crackers or in a sandwich.

1 large whole eggplant
1 large tomato
2–3 garlic cloves
¼ cup olive oil
juice of ½ lemon (or 2 tbsp vinegar)
sea salt, to taste
½ cup chopped fresh parsley

Preheat oven to 400°F (205°C).

Make 3 to 4 slits lengthwise in the eggplant, and insert garlic cloves into slits. Make some slits in the side of the tomato as well.

Place the eggplant and whole tomato on a lightly oiled baking sheet and bake until soft. (*Note:* the tomato may soften before the eggplant.) Remove the tomato when soft, then let the eggplant become soft and remove when done, about 45 minutes.

Remove baking pan from oven and let cool. Remove skins from the eggplant and tomato and discard skins.

In a food processor, blend the roasted eggplant and tomato, then add remaining ingredients and blend until smooth.

Makes 2 cups.

TARAMOSALATA (Fish Roe Spread)

Taramosalata is made during fasting periods, when meat and dairy are not eaten. Before the time of blenders and food processors, my grandmother would spend an hour pounding the fish roe with a stone mortar and pestle. Today, you can make taramosalata in a few minutes—but the secret to this recipe hasn't changed: great olive oil. High quality olive oil will add volumes in terms of flavor to this spread.

1 cup bread cubes (white, French, or whole wheat), soaked in water
½ cup fish roe
juice of 2 lemons
⅔ cup olive oil

Note: You can purchase fish roe at your local fishmonger or at most Mediterranean markets.

Squeeze out excess water from bread. Combine the roe with the bread in a blender. While blending, slowly add the lemon juice and olive oil until a smooth, thick dip is formed. Refrigerate to set. Serve on crusty bread.

Makes 2–2½ cups.

BALSAMIC FIG BRUSCHETTA WITH BLUE CHEESE FILLING

Every summer, the three fig trees in our back yard yield more fruit than we can eat. When buying fresh figs, look for ripe fruit that's soft to the touch.

1 tbsp butter
¼ cup balsamic vinegar
2 tsp brown sugar
6 fresh figs, cut into quarters

Filling:
¾ cup blue cheese, crumbled
⅓ cup mascarpone (or ricotta) cheese
1 tbsp chopped fresh parsley
¼ tsp freshly ground black pepper

Bruschetta:
1 baguette, sliced in
   1-in (2.5-cm) thick pieces
3 tbsp olive oil
3 garlic cloves

Preheat oven to 375°F (190°C).

Combine butter, vinegar, and brown sugar in a medium frying pan on medium heat. Stir in figs and sauté for 5–10 minutes, or until lightly browned. Remove from heat and set aside.

Combine blue and mascarpone cheeses, parsley, and pepper in a small mixing bowl.

Place baguette slices on a baking sheet. Brush with olive oil. Bake for about 5 minutes until lightly browned (or under broiler on high for no more than 2–3 minutes). Remove from oven and rub with garlic.

Set oven to broil. Place a spoonful of the cheese mixture on each slice of bread and top with a fig. Place under broiler for 1 minute. Serve warm.

Makes 18–24 servings.

{ *Want to try something new? Do as Basil does: Place a walnut half in a fresh fig and dehydrate, dip it in good quality dark chocolate, and then freeze.*

FETA CHEESE-STUFFED HOT BANANA PEPPERS

This dish tastes best when peppers are in season. Serve hot or cold.

10 hot banana peppers
½ cup crumbled feta cheese
1 fresh tomato, puréed (or ½ cup fresh tomato sauce, unseasoned)
1 tsp dried oregano
½ cup olive oil

Cut the tops off the banana peppers, then core and seed them. Set the tops aside. Combine the feta cheese, tomato purée, and oregano in a medium mixing bowl. Stuff this filling into the hollowed-out banana peppers. Place the tops back onto peppers (use a toothpick to hold the tops in place).

Heat the olive oil in a medium frying pan on medium (too high and you'll burn the peppers' skins too quickly). Add peppers and sauté on all sides for 2–4 minutes or until peppers are tender and their skins turn golden brown.

Makes 4–6 servings.

THREE EASY ACCOMPANIMENTS TO KEBABS

My father loved kebabs (p. 90). They are best served with these fresh and savory side dishes—and a glass of wine. Don't forget the pita (p. 169) and hummus (p. 26)!

Onions

1 large onion, thinly sliced
½ tsp cayenne pepper
½ cup parsley

Mix onion, cayenne pepper, and parsley in a serving bowl.

Tomatoes

4 large tomatoes, thickly sliced
1–2 tbsp olive oil, or to taste
sea salt, to taste

Place sliced tomatoes on an oiled baking pan. Brush tomatoes on both sides with olive oil and season with salt. Grill on each side until lightly browned (about 3–5 minutes). Remove from oven.

Potatoes

4–6 medium potatoes, sliced like French fries
¼ cup olive oil
sea salt, to taste
fresh or dried oregano, to taste

Preheat oven to 400°F (205°C).

Mix potatoes with olive oil in a baking pan. Toss well. Bake until potatoes are tender and lightly browned, about 25 minutes. Remove from oven. Season with sea salt and oregano.

Makes 4–6 servings.

GRILLED VEGETABLES

Grilled vegetables are a staple in any Greek kitchen. Serve hot or cold on an anti-pasto platter with cheese, olives, marinated artichokes, and sliced meats, or as a side to any meat or fish dish.

1 large eggplant, sliced ¼-in (6-mm) thick
3 medium-large zucchinis, sliced ¼-in (6-mm) thick
2 green bell peppers, seeded and cut in quarters
2 red bell peppers, seeded and cut in quarters
1 large tomato, sliced
about ½–1 cup olive oil
sea salt, to taste
1 tsp garlic powder (optional)
1 tsp fresh or dried basil (optional)
1 tsp fresh or dried oregano (optional)
1 tsp fresh or dried thyme (optional)

Set oven to broil (or start barbecue).

If using the oven, place vegetables on a baking sheet. Brush vegetables with olive oil (enough so the surface is covered) and lightly salt on both sides 45 minutes before broiling or grilling; this will enhance the flavor. Sprinkle with garlic and herbs, if desired. (Rub the herbs in your hands before sprinkling over veggies in order to release their aromatic, flavorful oils.)

Grill or broil vegetables for 2–5 minutes on each side, or until flesh is lightly browned. Serve hot or cold.

Makes 8–12 servings.

ARTICHOKES WITH DILL MUSTARD SAUCE

A tasty appetizer with a tangy twist. You can't go wrong with garlic, lemon, fresh dill, and artichokes. Did I mention garlic?

2 large artichoke hearts
juice of 1 lemon
sea salt, to taste

Sauce:
juice of 2 lemons
¼ cup olive oil
½ tsp dried mustard
1 garlic clove
1 tsp chopped fresh dill
sea salt, to taste
freshly ground black pepper, to taste

Dip clean artichoke hearts in juice of 1 lemon to prevent discoloration. Place in a medium saucepan on high and cover with salted water. Boil for 30–40 minutes, or until artichokes are tender. Remove artichokes from saucepan.

Combine lemon juice, olive oil, dried mustard, garlic, fresh dill, salt, and pepper in a blender until smooth. Place the cooked artichokes on a serving platter and drizzle with the dill-mustard sauce. Serve warm.

Makes 2 servings.

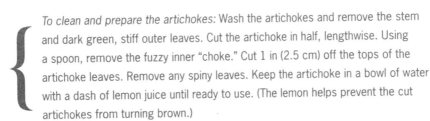

To clean and prepare the artichokes: Wash the artichokes and remove the stem and dark green, stiff outer leaves. Cut the artichoke in half, lengthwise. Using a spoon, remove the fuzzy inner "choke." Cut 1 in (2.5 cm) off the tops of the artichoke leaves. Remove any spiny leaves. Keep the artichoke in a bowl of water with a dash of lemon juice until ready to use. (The lemon helps prevent the cut artichokes from turning brown.)

MELITZANOKEFTEDES (Eggplant Balls)

A lovely vegetarian snack or appetizer sure to wow your guests. For a richer flavor, first roast the garlic cloves.

2 medium eggplants
1 large onion, grated
1–2 garlic cloves, minced
½ cup finely chopped fresh parsley
½ cup grated Parmesan cheese
2 eggs
1 cup breadcrumbs
sea salt, to taste
freshly ground black pepper, to taste
¾ cup olive oil

Preheat oven to 400°F (205°C).

Cut slits into the eggplants and place on a lightly oiled baking sheet. Bake for 30–45 minutes, or until the eggplants are soft to the touch. Let cool. Remove and discard skins. Squeeze eggplant flesh to remove any excess water, then mash in a medium mixing bowl.

Add onion, garlic, parsley, Parmesan cheese, eggs, and breadcrumbs and mix well. Add salt and pepper. Knead all ingredients and shape mixture into 1-in (2.5-cm) balls.

Heat olive oil in a large frying pan on medium to high, and fry eggplant balls for 3–5 minutes, or until golden brown. Place cooked melitzanokeftedes on paper towel to absorb excess oil. Serve hot or cold.

Makes 4 servings.

ROASTED RED BELL PEPPERS

Chef Jean-Francis Quaglia, Provence Marinaside, Vancouver, BC

This is the one antipasti dish we really look forward to when we visit our family in France. Roasted red bell peppers are included at almost every French dinner table as an appetizer. The bell peppers in France have an incredible sweetness, so we suggest making this dish in the summer when North American bell peppers taste best. Using extra virgin olive oil is the key to making this dish perfectly delicious!

6 large red bell peppers
5 garlic cloves, chopped
1 cup chopped fresh parsley
sea salt, to taste
freshly ground black pepper, to taste
½ cup olive oil

Set oven to broil.

Place whole peppers on lightly oiled baking sheet and broil for about 25 minutes, turning peppers occasionally, until they are charred all over.

Remove peppers from oven, place in a bowl, and cover with plastic wrap to keep them moist until they are cool enough to handle. Peel off peppers' skins, cut in half lengthwise, discard seeds, and slice lengthwise into 1-in (2.5-cm) strips.

Return strips to bowl, and add garlic, parsley, salt, pepper, and olive oil. Mix until ingredients are well combined, using a spoon or—even better—your hands. Check seasoning and serve on a platter with olives, crackers, and cheese.

Makes 4 servings.

FETA WITH HONEY ROSEMARY OLIVE OIL DRESSING

Tony Minichiello, Northwest Culinary Academy of Vancouver, Vancouver, BC

You can infuse the honey in this recipe with any herb you like—lavender, thyme, or even lemon or orange peel. You can also substitute mild blue cheese or Cambozola for the feta. Top with roasted chopped almonds or hazelnuts, diced fresh figs, or pomegranate seeds.

1 lb (454g) feta cheese, cut into ½-in (1-cm) slices

Honey Rosemary Dressing:
¼ cup good quality honey
¼ cup water
1 small sprig rosemary, roughly chopped
coarsely cracked black peppercorns
¼ cup olive oil

Combine honey and water in a small saucepan on medium heat. Simmer honey-water with rosemary and peppercorns on low heat until reduced by half (or back to the consistency of honey).

Take off the heat and, while still hot, whisk in the olive oil. Dressing will separate slightly. Pour over sliced feta square. Garnish as desired and serve warm.

Makes about 1 cup.

SAGANAKI (Fried Cheese)

A traditional Greek appetizer, made with Kefalotiri, a salty Greek sheep's milk cheese, available at most Mediterranean delis. Make sure you have plenty of fresh lemon juice on hand to squeeze over the cheese just before serving (or cut up a lemon and let the guests do this themselves); it really brings out the flavor!

1 egg
2 slices Kefalotiri cheese, ¼-in (⅔-cm) thick
⅓ cup flour
¾ cup olive oil
juice of 1 lemon

Beat egg in a mixing bowl. Dip cheese slices in the egg and then in the flour. Repeat: dip the cheese in the egg and then in the flour.

Heat olive oil in a frying pan on medium-low heat. Add cheese slices and fry for 2–5 minutes on each side, or until golden brown. Drizzle with freshly squeezed lemon juice and serve warm.

Makes 2 servings.

ESCARGOT IN TOMATO–WINE SAUCE

This recipe reminds me of my dear mother; she used to make this dish when I was a child. My friends would ask what she was stirring in the pot, which sounded like a soup full of rocks! Of course, they were escargot in the shell. My friends loved eating whatever my mother made, and this dish was no exception.

¼ cup olive oil
3 large onions, finely chopped
3 garlic cloves, minced
2 lbs (1 kg) fresh escargot (in shell), rinsed well
½–1 cup red wine
2 medium tomatoes, puréed
2 tbsp finely chopped fresh anise (or fennel bulb)
sea salt, to taste
freshly ground black pepper, to taste

Heat olive oil in a medium saucepan on medium. Add onions and garlic and sauté for about 5 minutes or until onions are soft and lightly browned. Add escargot and wine, increase the heat, and bring to a boil. Add tomato and anise, and reduce heat to medium-low. Season with salt and pepper and simmer on low for 1 hour, stirring occasionally or until sauce has thickened.

Serve with crusty bread to hold the escargot and mop up the delicious sauce.

Makes 4–8 servings.

ESCARGOT WITH ROSEMARY

In Greece, escargot are known as saligaria, and they can be found in dry shrubbery throughout the countryside. After picking our saligaria, we leave them in a covered basket with some flour and a few branches to start the cleansing process. But you can buy them in a can—don't eat the ones from your garden! Serve this appetizer with crusty bread and a glass of good red wine.

3 tbsp olive oil
2 cups sliced button mushrooms
3 tbsp olive oil
4 garlic cloves
1 can of 24–36 escargot (without shell), rinsed well
3 tbsp dried rosemary (or 3 sprigs fresh rosemary)
½ tsp sea salt
freshly ground black pepper, to taste
3 tbsp wine vinegar
¼ cup red (or white) wine
¼ tsp dried marjoram
½ tsp dried thyme
1 tsp flour

Heat olive oil in a medium saucepan on medium to high. Add sliced mushrooms and sauté for 5–10 minutes, or until softened. Remove from heat and set aside.

In a new saucepan, heat olive oil on medium heat, add garlic and sauté on low until fragrant. Stir in escargot, rosemary, salt, pepper, and the cooked mushrooms.

Reduce heat to low, and add wine vinegar, wine, marjoram, thyme, and flour. Simmer for 10–15 minutes.

Makes 4 servings.

OYSTERS CAPARI

Oysters Capari (Greek for capers) is a simple seafood appetizer for two. Place the steamed oysters on the shell (or on lettuce leaves) for presentation and garnish as desired.

12 fresh oysters
¼ cup olive oil
juice of 1 lemon
sea salt, to taste
1 tbsp capers
4 small sprigs fresh parsley, to garnish

Wash the oyster shells to remove any debris. Place 4–5 cups water in a double boiler and bring to a boil. Place oyster shells in the top part of the pot and steam until the shells have opened enough to shuck. Remove from heat and strain.

Remove the steamed oysters from their shells and arrange on a serving platter.

Combine the olive oil, lemon juice, salt, and capers in a small bowl. Place the steamed oysters on a plate of lettuce leaves, pour sauce over oysters, and garnish with parsley. Serve immediately.

Makes 2 servings.

TARAMOKEFTEDES (Fish Roe Rissoles)

Rissoles are small croquettes or cakes. Traditionally, taramokeftedes are made while fasting during Lent. You can serve these any time of year as an appetizer or side with green salad. (Fish roe can be found at your fishmonger or most Mediterranean delis.)

2 large potatoes
½ cup tarama (fish roe)
½ cup finely chopped green onions
2 tbsp finely chopped fresh dill
2 tbsp finely chopped fresh parsley
sea salt, to taste
freshly ground black pepper, to taste
1–2 cups breadcrumbs (or flour)
1 cup olive oil
juice of 1 lemon

Peel and cut potatoes into ½-in (1-cm) cubes and boil in a large pot of water until cooked. Strain and set aside.

Blend the tarama in a mixing bowl using a hand mixer (or in a food processor). Blend in cooked potato, green onions, dill, parsley, salt, and pepper.

Shape mixture into 1-in (2.5-cm) balls and roll in breadcrumbs or flour. Heat olive oil in a large frying on medium to high and add the taramokeftedes. Fry on each side for 3–5 minutes, or until lightly browned and crisp on the outside. Garnish with freshly squeezed lemon juice.

Makes 15–20 cakes.

SMELTS IN WHITE WINE WITH SAVORY SAVORO SAUCE

Basil loves to fish. When the girls were young, we would take them to the beach and throw out our fishing nets to catch smelts. We would come home late at night and prepare smelt appetizers for us all to enjoy. Nothing like a fresh catch.

1 lb (½ kg) fresh smelts, cleaned, with heads removed
sea salt, to taste
3 tbsp olive oil
1 onion, finely chopped (about 1 cup)
½ cup coarsely chopped fresh parsley
sea salt, to taste
freshly ground black pepper, to taste
juice from 3 lemons
1–2 cups dry white wine
hot chili pepper flakes (optional)

Salt the smelts and set aside. Heat olive oil in a medium saucepan on medium-high. Add onions and parsley, and sauté until onions are translucent.

Add the whole smelts, salt, pepper, lemon juice, and enough white wine to cover the fish. Simmer for about 20–30 minutes. Serve hot or cold, topped with Savory Savoro Sauce (see recipe following) and garnished with chili pepper flakes, if desired.

(*Note:* After adding smelts to saucepan, you can bake them in a 350°F [180°C] oven for 20–30 minutes instead of cooking them on the stove.)

Savory Savoro Sauce:
3 tbsp olive oil
½ cup flour
⅓ cup wine or white vinegar
1–2 tsp water
1 tbsp finely chopped fresh rosemary
sea salt, to taste
freshly ground black pepper, to taste

Heat olive oil in a small frying pan on low. Stir in flour to make a smooth paste. While stirring, mix in the vinegar and water until it has a creamy consistency. Add rosemary and salt. Simmer for 5 minutes.

Remove from heat and season with pepper and more salt, if necessary. Strain sauce to remove any lumps. Pour over smelts before serving.

Makes 4–6 servings.

AVOCADO CRAB CAKES

Avocado coupled with crab makes a great appetizer for any dinner party. You can serve these hot or cold.

2 medium zucchini, grated
sea salt, to taste
3 green onions, finely chopped
1 avocado, mashed
1 cup crab meat
¼ cup finely chopped fresh dill
½ red pepper, finely chopped (optional)
¼ cup finely chopped fresh parsley or cilantro
1 tsp sea salt
freshly ground black pepper, to taste
1 whole egg (optional)
1 cup breadcrumbs or flour, seasoned with sea salt and pepper
½ cup olive oil

Mix grated zucchini and salt in a mixing bowl, then strain, squeezing out as much liquid as you can.

Combine onions, mashed avocado, crab meat, dill, red pepper (if using), parsley or cilantro, salt, pepper, and egg until well mixed. Form mixture into 1½–2-in (4–5-cm) round patties. Dredge patties in breadcrumbs or flour, tapping off any excess.

Heat olive oil in a saucepan on medium-high heat. Cook crabcakes for 3–5 minutes on each side, or until browned. Serve these appetizers warm or cold with garlic aioli (p. 25).

Makes approximately 12 crab cakes.

Salmon à la Méditerranée (page 124) and Seasonal Greens with Lemon & Olive Oil (page 138)

Garides Youvetsi Me Feta (page 130)

Tzatziki (page 28), Tirokafteri (page 27), Melitzanosalata (page 31), and Basil Pesto (page 24)

Feta Cheese-Stuffed Hot Banana Peppers (page 34)

Grilled Vegetables (page 36)

Greek Salad (page 58), Tabouleh (page 66)

ARUGULA, PEACH, & GOAT CHEESE SALAD
WITH CARAMLIZED PECANS

ASPARAGUS SALAD

AVOCADO, CUCUMBER, & TOMATO SALAD

CLASSIC CAESAR SALAD

BLUE CHEESE CAESAR SALAD

CUCUMBER DILL SALAD

DILL BEAN SALAD

*— Salads &
Salad Dressings*

FENNEL SALAD

GREEK SALAD

HERBS & GREENS WITH VINE TOMATO &
OLIVE OIL VINAIGRETTE

GREEN TOMATO & POTATO SALAD

SALTED COD & POTATO SALAD

SEARED SCALLOPS

SEARED TUNA SALAD WITH KALAMATA
OLIVE TAPENADE

TABOULEH (Parsley & Couscous Salad)

ARUGULA, PEACH, & GOAT CHEESE SALAD WITH CARAMELIZED PECANS

The peppery taste of arugula complements the fresh olive oil, soft goat cheese, and sweet crunchiness of the pecans. It's heaven on a plate.

2 tbsp white or brown sugar
½ cup pecans
4 cups fresh arugula,
2 cups fresh baby spinach, (optional)
3 tbsp sunflower seeds
1 peach, peeled and cut in thin slices
¼ cup crumbled goat cheese
sea salt, to taste
freshly ground black pepper, to taste
juice of ½ orange
1 tsp balsamic vinegar
3–4 tbsp olive oil

Add a few drops of water to a small saucepan on medium heat, then add the sugar. Once the sugar has dissolved, add the pecans, stirring until sugar has caramelized and completely coated the pecans. (Be careful not to burn the sugar.) Remove from heat.

Toss all ingredients (including the dressing) in a large salad bowl. Top with pecans.

Makes 4–6 servings.

ASPARAGUS SALAD

A great accompaniment to any meat or seafood dish. Just don't overcook the asparagus; it's best on the crunchy side.

1 lb (½ kg) asparagus
3 tbsp olive oil
1½ tbsp white vinegar
½ tsp oregano
½ tsp basil
½ tsp rosemary
1 garlic clove, minced
sea salt, to taste
freshly ground black pepper, to taste
mixed greens
2–3 tbsp grated Parmesan cheese, as garnish

To blanch asparagus: Add asparagus to a large pot of boiling water for 3–4 minutes. Drain, rinse under cold water, and set aside.

Place blanched asparagus in a glass baking pan or deep serving dish. Combine the rest of the ingredients (except for the mixed greens and cheese) in a small bowl, mix well, and pour mixture over the asparagus. Marinate overnight (or for 3–4 hours) in the refrigerator.

Serve asparagus on a bed of mixed greens topped with a generous sprinkle of Parmesan cheese.

Makes 6–8 servings.

AVOCADO, CUCUMBER, & TOMATO SALAD

Make sure your avocado is soft and ripe. Try heirloom tomato varieties, when in season, to add new flavors and colors to your salad. Serve with crusty bread.

2 large ripe tomatoes, cut in wedges
1 ripe avocado, cubed
½ cup coarsely chopped fresh parsley
1 cup sliced cucumber
3 green onions, chopped
1 garlic clove, grated or crushed
¼ cup olive oil
juice of 1 lemon
sea salt, to taste
4 romaine lettuce leaves

Combine all ingredients (except the lettuce leaves) in a large bowl and mix well. Place a lettuce leaf on each of 4 plates and mound the salad on top of it.

Makes 4 servings.

CLASSIC CAESAR SALAD

Garlic. Garlic. Garlic. The more, the better! Use the dressing on your salad, as a dip, or on baked or grilled fish.

2 garlic cloves, crushed
1 anchovy (optional)
1 egg yolk, coddled (see p. 25)
juice of 1 lemon
3 tbsp olive oil

½ cup grated Parmesan cheese
sea salt, to taste
freshly ground black pepper, to taste
1 head romaine lettuce, torn into bite-
   sized pieces

Combine all ingredients, except lettuce, in a food processor and blend until creamy. Refrigerate until ready to serve. Toss well with romaine lettuce leaves, and top with croutons (see recipe, below). Serve immediately.

Makes ½–1 cup.

Croutons:
¼ cup olive oil
3–4 cups bread cubes
(about 1 in/2.5 cm square)
1–2 garlic cloves, minced
sea salt, to taste

freshly ground black pepper, to taste
1 tsp dried basil
1 tsp dried oregano
3 tbsp grated Parmesan cheese
1 tbsp balsamic vinegar (optional)

Preheat oven to 375°F (190°C).

Heat oil in a large frying pan on medium-high. Add bread, garlic, seasoning and herbs. Lightly fry the cubes, turning and stirring once or twice so that all sides are equally browned, for 2–5 minutes.

Remove from pan and place croutons on a baking sheet. Sprinkle croutons with Parmesan cheese (and balsamic vinegar, if using) and bake for 5–10 minutes or until golden brown. Remove from oven and let cool. Toss over salad.

Makes 4 servings.

BLUE CHEESE CAESAR SALAD

Blue cheese + crispy romaine leaves = delicious. For a bit more kick, add more garlic. Also great as a dip!

1 egg yolk, coddled (see p. 25)
2 garlic cloves
½ cup olive oil
juice of 1 lemon
1 tbsp Dijon mustard
½ cup blue cheese
1 tsp sea salt
romaine lettuce leaves, torn into bite-sized pieces

Combine all ingredients except lettuce in a food processor, blending until smooth. Refrigerate dressing until needed. Pour over romaine lettuce or salad greens and toss well.

Makes 1½ cups dressing.

CUCUMBER DILL SALAD

An easy salad to make for any occasion, and a refreshing accompaniment to grilled meats or fish. For a bigger flavor punch, use balsamic instead of white vinegar.

8–12 baby cucumbers, cut in ¼-in (6-mm) pieces
½-1 cup chopped fresh dill
3–4 tbsp olive oil
1 tbsp white vinegar
sea salt, to taste

Combine all ingredients in a large salad bowl. Toss well and serve.

Makes 4–6 servings.

DILL BEAN SALAD

A Koutalianos family favorite and a perfect side to baked and/or fried calamari (p. 135) or fish (p. 116).

2½ cups white beans, any kind, cooked (or 2 14-oz/398-mL cans of white beans)
½ cup chopped fresh dill
1 red onion, finely chopped
1 green pepper, seeded and cut in thin strips
1–2 garlic cloves, minced
juice of 1 lemon
sea salt, to taste
freshly ground black pepper, to taste

Combine all ingredients in a large salad bowl. Toss well and serve at room temperature.

Makes 6–8 servings.

FENNEL SALAD

Fennel (also known as anise) is crispy, light, and fresh, with a delicious flavor similar to licorice.

1 large fennel bulb and green tops
½ garlic clove, finely minced
½ cup olive oil
juice of 1 lemon
sea salt, to taste

Remove the stalk and coarse outer sections of the fennel (use only the tender parts) and slice finely. Combine with remainder of ingredients and toss well.

Makes 2–4 servings.

GREEK SALAD

A few secrets to making a great Greek salad: Use room temperature ripe tomatoes, as refrigerated tomatoes don't taste as good. Also, be aware that the feta cheese and olives are quite salty, so add salt sparingly, if at all, to this recipe.

4 large tomatoes, cut into eighths
1 green bell pepper, cut in strips
1 medium onion, cut into long thin strips
1 cucumber, sliced in half lengthwise and chopped into ½-in (1-cm) pieces (optional)
¾–1 cup crumbled feta cheese
5–10 Kalamata olives, whole (or more, or none, as desired)
¼ cup olive oil
1 tsp dried oregano
1 tsp fresh mint
sea salt, to taste

Combine all ingredients in a large salad bowl and toss well. Serve with crusty bread.

Makes 4–6 servings.

HERBS & GREENS WITH VINE TOMATO AND OLIVE OIL VINAIGRETTE

Chef Liana Robberecht, Calgary Petroleum Club, Calgary, Alberta

Serve as an appetizer or as a light, refreshing side salad. To make this a heartier meal, add cooked seafood, chicken, or beef.

2 large ripe vine tomatoes
1–2 tbsp olive oil
1 shallot, minced
1 tsp honey
2 tbsp rice wine vinegar (or to taste)
½ cup olive oil
sea salt, to taste

fresh cracked pepper, to taste
zest of 1 lemon
½ head butter leaf lettuce
2 sprigs fresh basil
2 sprigs fresh tarragon
1 bunch fresh baby arugula
2 sprigs fresh dill
2 large tomatoes, sliced
4 oz (115 g) Kalamata olives

Continued next page.

Blanch the tomatoes in a pot of boiling water for 3–5 minutes. Remove tomatoes and rinse under cold water. Peel and seed.

In a small frying pan on medium heat, add the olive oil and sauté the shallots for 2–3 minutes, or until tender. Let cool and set aside.

Combine blanched tomatoes, shallots, honey, and vinegar in a blender. While blending, slowly add olive oil. Once blended, pour into mixing bowl, using a whisk. Add salt, pepper, and lemon zest. Taste and adjust seasoning.

Combine washed lettuce and herbs in a large salad bowl, then arrange onto plate. Garnish with sliced vine tomatoes and olives.

Warm dressing briefly in a small saucepan then pour over greens and garnish, and serve immediately.

Makes 4 servings.

GREEN TOMATO & POTATO SALAD

Wondering what to do with green tomatoes at the end of the growing season?
Serve this salad either hot or cold to accompany grilled meat or fish.

2 large potatoes, cut into small (1-in/2.5-cm) cubes
6 green tomatoes, cut into quarters
1 cup green bell pepper, seeded and diced finely
1 tbsp vinegar
1 garlic clove, crushed
3 tbsp olive oil
sea salt, to taste
freshly ground black pepper, to taste

Bring a large pot of lightly salted water to a boil. Add potatoes and cook for 5–7 minutes, until almost tender (can be pierced with a fork, but aren't yet soft). Add tomatoes and green pepper and boil for another 5–7 minutes, until potatoes are soft. Remove from heat and drain vegetables.

Combine the cooked vegetables with the remainder of the ingredients in a large bowl and toss well.

Makes 4–6 servings.

SALT COD & POTATO SALAD

My father loved this dish. The salt cod and olive oil give it a unique flavor. Salt cod is cod that has been dried and preserved in salt; once rehydrated, the fish is white and flaky. It can be found in Mediterranean markets.

1 lb (½ kg) salt cod
4 large potatoes, cubed
¼ cup chopped fresh parsley
3–4 garlic cloves, crushed
juice of 1 lemon
¼ cup olive oil
sea salt, to taste
freshly ground black pepper, to taste
1 lemon, cut in wedges

Soak the cod in water for 6–8 hours to soften the fish and remove the salty taste. Drain soaking water and replace with fresh water several times during the soaking process, if possible.

The next day, add cod to a large pot of boiling water, cook for about 20 minutes or until tender, strain water, and flake fish into small bite-sized chunks.

Bring a large pot of water to a boil and add cubed potatoes. Cook for about 20–30 minutes or until potatoes are tender but not mushy.

Combine the cooked cod and potatoes with the parsley, garlic, lemon juice, and olive oil in a large bowl and mix well. Add salt and pepper to taste. Cover and let stand for 15–20 minutes before serving. Serve with lemon wedges to squeeze over each portion.

Makes 4–6 servings.

SEARED SCALLOPS

James Walt, Araxi Restaurant, Whistler, BC

The rich flavor of extra virgin olive oil and the sweetness of fresh scallops make this a mouth-watering appetizer.

2 tbsp extra virgin olive oil
¼ tsp curry powder
1 tsp sea salt, crushed, to taste
8 medium-large fresh scallops (cleaned and with abductor muscle removed)

In a sauté pan, heat 2 tbsp of oil on medium heat (the oil should not be heated for too long). Blend curry powder and salt together and lightly season the scallops on both sides. Place in the sauté pan and cook until golden on both sides, about 1–2 minutes per side depending on the thickness of the scallops. Serve right away with Maple Mustard Vinaigrette (recipe follows).

Makes 2 servings.

Maple Mustard Vinaigrette

¼ cup grainy seed mustard
1 tbsp hot water
⅓ cup maple vinegar
⅓ cup extra virgin olive oil
sea salt, to taste
white pepper, to taste

Place mustard in a stainless steel bowl, and slowly whisk in the hot water and maple vinegar. Slowly whisk in the olive oil. Taste and season lightly with salt and pepper.

Makes 1 cup.

SEARED TUNA SALAD WITH KALAMATA OLIVE TAPENADE

Chef Lisa Ahier, SoBo Restaurant, Tofino, BC

A blend of West Coast cuisine with Mediterranean accents, this dish is a palette pleaser. Wherever you live, buy fresh and buy local.

8 whole green beans
4 quail eggs (or 2 chicken eggs)
1 tbsp white vinegar
4 medium potatoes (Yukon gold recommended)
2 tbsp olive oil
1 lb (½ kg) tuna loin, cut into 4 equal portions
8 tbsp Kalamata olive tapenade (p. 29)
2 tbsp olive oil
1 onion, thinly sliced
8 cherry tomatoes
8 anchovies
8 oz (225g) spring mix salad greens

Champagne Tarragon Dressing:
2 tbsp champagne vinegar
1 tbsp honey
1 tsp mustard
6 sprigs of tarragon, minced
sea salt, to taste
freshly ground black pepper, to taste
6 tbsp extra virgin olive oil

Bring a medium pot of lightly salted water to a boil, add green beans, and blanch for 1–2 minutes. Then immediately plunge the green beans into a bowl of ice water.

Carefully place quail (or chicken) eggs in simmering water with 1 tbsp vinegar (this will make the eggs easier to peel) for 2–3 minutes. Once cooked, strain the soft-boiled eggs into a colander and rinse under cool water to stop the eggs from cooking further. Peel, slice in half (or in quarters if using chicken eggs), and set aside.

Steam potatoes whole for approximately 20–30 minutes, until they can be pierced with a fork, then slice into ¼-in (6-mm) rounds.

Heat olive oil in a large sauté pan on medium-high. Just before the oil reaches smoking point, place all four tuna portions in the pan. Sear tuna for 10–15 seconds, then flip and repeat. Remove from pan, and allow tuna to rest for approximately 5 minutes before slicing each portion into ½-in (1-cm) thick pieces.

Add olive oil to small sauce pan on medium heat. Add onion and caramelize. To prepare the Champagne Tarragon dressing, combine vinegar, honey, mustard, tarragon, salt, and pepper, then slowly whisk in oil until emulsified.

Toss green beans, eggs, tomatoes, anchovies, potatoes, onion and spring mix in Champagne Tarragon dressing. Fan out the tuna slices onto salad and top off with Kalamata olive tapenade.

Makes 4 servings.

TABOULEH (Parsley & Couscous Salad)

A traditional Middle Eastern salad, tabouleh is light and fresh, and goes well with fish and grilled meats and vegetables.

1 cup couscous
4 cups coarsely chopped fresh parsley
1 small onion, finely chopped
1 tomato, finely chopped
juice of 1 lemon
sea salt, to taste
freshly ground black pepper, to taste
¼ cup olive oil

Bring 1 cup of water to a boil and add couscous. Bring back to a boil, then remove from heat, cover, and let stand for 5 minutes. Combine couscous with remainder of ingredients in a large bowl. Toss well.

Makes 4–6 servings.

REVITHOSOUPA (Chickpea Soup)

FAKI (Lentil Soup)

FASOLADA (Romano Bean Soup)

FASOLIA ME MARATHO (Fennel & Bean Soup)

MINESTRONE SOUP

VEGETABLE SOUP WITH ORZO

PSAROSOUPA (Fish Chowder)

SEARED SCALLOP & SPOT PRAWN GAZPACHO

Soups & Stews

HEIRLOOM TOMATO GAZPACHO WITH SHRIMP,
CHEESE CURD, & BASIL

MAYIRITSA (Traditional Easter Soup)

OXTAIL BARLEY SOUP

YOUVARLAKIA (Meatball Soup)

ARTICHOKE & VEGETABLE STEW

EUROPEAN STEW

LAMB & FRESH GREEN BEAN STEW

STIFATHO (Venison & Pearl Onion) STEW

REVITHOSOUPA (Chickpea Soup)

Basil loves this soup, and so do I—it's healthy and tasty. My youngest daughter Evangeline is a vegetarian, so we omit the meat for her but never the flavor!

¼ cup olive oil

1 lb (½ kg) organic beef or veal, cubed

2 garlic cloves, minced or crushed

sea salt, to taste

1 cup cooked chickpeas (garbanzo beans)

  (or 1 14-oz/398-mL can)

½ cup uncooked brown rice

¼ cup finely chopped fresh parsley

freshly ground black pepper, to taste

Roux:

1 tbsp flour

½ cup soup stock

juice of 1 lemon

Heat olive oil in a large (3-qt/L) pot on medium. Add meat and sauté until browned. Add garlic, salt, pepper, and about 6 cups of water and bring to a boil.

After 15 minutes, reduce heat to low and simmer for 15–20 minutes or until meat is tender. Add cooked chickpeas and rice and simmer for another 15–20 minutes or until rice is cooked.

Add parsley and remove from heat. Remove ½ cup soup stock from the pot and set aside.

Prepare the roux by slowly adding reserved soup stock to flour, then adding lemon juice and whisking or stirring until smooth. Add this mixture to the soup; it will help thicken the soup and give it a wonderful lemon flavor. Season each serving with a little more freshly ground black pepper.

Makes 4–6 servings.

{ *If you want to cook dried chickpeas, start by soaking them in water overnight, then drain. Bring 3–4 parts fresh water to a boil and add 1 part chickpeas. Cook for 1–2 hours, or until tender.*

FAKI (Lentil Soup)

Faki is a traditional Greek soup made with lentils. It's simple to make, and very tasty. Serve with baked or grilled fish. (Tip: Make sure to wash your lentils well before cooking to remove any tiny stones.)

2 cups lentils, washed
1 large onion, finely chopped
3 garlic cloves, finely chopped
¼ cup olive oil
1 bay leaf
1 tsp dried thyme
1 tsp sea salt
½ tsp freshly ground black pepper
¼ cup uncooked white rice (optional)
1 fresh tomato, puréed (optional)
white vinegar, to taste

Bring a large pot of water to a boil. Add lentils, onions, garlic, olive oil, spices and about 6 cups water. Add rice and tomato, if desired. Simmer on medium heat until lentils are soft and the stock is thick, about 30–45 minutes.

Just before serving, add a dollop of vinegar.

Makes 4–6 servings.

FASOLADA (Romano Bean Soup)

Romano beans are a flat snap bean. Fasolada is a hearty traditional Greek soup and makes a great comfort food for cold winter nights when served with crusty bread.

3 tbsp olive oil
1 medium onion, chopped
2 garlic cloves, minced
1½ cups finely chopped celery
2–3 large carrots, thinly sliced
1½ cups crushed tomatoes
1 tsp sea salt
½ tsp black pepper
2 cups cooked (or canned) romano beans

If using dried beans: Soak dried beans in water overnight. Next, bring 4–6 cups of water to a boil and add beans. Cook on medium-high heat for 1 hour, or until beans are tender. Drain and follow recipe.

Heat olive oil in a large pot on medium. Add onions and garlic and sauté until translucent. Add the celery and carrots and cook for 10 minutes or until vegetables are slightly tender. Add 6 cups water, crushed tomatoes, salt, and pepper. Bring to a boil. Add the cooked beans, and reduce heat to medium. Simmer for 30 minutes.

Makes 4–6 servings.

FASOLIA ME MARATHO (Fennel & Bean Soup)

A flavorful Greek soup. Don't forget the feta cheese!

½ cup olive oil
2 large onions, finely chopped
1 fennel bulb, finely chopped
3 stalks celery, finely chopped
3 cups cooked (or canned) pinto beans
4 cups crushed tomatoes
sea salt, to taste
freshly ground black pepper, to taste
⅓ cup crumbled feta cheese

Heat olive oil in a large pot on medium. Add onions, fennel, and celery. Sauté
until onions are translucent, about 5–8 minutes. Reduce heat to medium and add
beans, tomatoes, salt, and pepper. Simmer until soup is thick, 30–45 minutes.
(If soup is too thick, add a little water).

Top with crumbled feta cheese.

Makes 4–6 servings.

MINESTRONE SOUP

Minestrone, a staple of Italian cooking, has many variations, but always includes a grain (here, pasta) and a legume (here, kidney beans). Vegetarians can use vegetable stock instead of chicken and omit the meat. Otherwise, the shredded chicken or turkey makes for a heartier meal. Just don't overcook the macaroni!

½ cup olive oil

2 cups chopped onions

3 stalks celery, finely chopped

3 carrots, finely chopped

2 cups chopped fresh green beans (1-in/2.5-cm pieces)

1 medium zucchini, cut into quarters lengthwise and cubed

1 cup cooked (or canned) kidney beans

1 cup crushed tomatoes

1 tsp dried basil

1 tsp dried oregano

1½ tsp sea salt

½ cup finely chopped broad leaf parsley

1 bay leaf

8–10 cups chicken (or vegetable) stock

2 cups elbow macaroni or broad noodles

1½–2 cups cooked chicken or turkey meat, diced or shredded (optional)

freshly ground black pepper, to taste

2–3 tbsp grated Parmesan cheese (to garnish)

Heat olive oil in a large pot on medium. Add onions, celery, carrots, green beans, and zucchini. Sauté until onions are translucent. Add cooked beans, tomatoes, spices, and stock.

Reduce heat to medium-low and simmer until vegetables are cooked, 15–20 minutes. Add noodles and simmer for another 10 minutes. (If soup is too thick, you can add water to dilute.) Add cooked meat if using. Season each serving with black pepper and garnish with Parmesan cheese.

Makes 6–8 servings.

VEGETABLE SOUP WITH ORZO

This is hearty soup all vegetarians will love and one my daughter Evangeline can't go without. Packed full of vitamins! Serve with Yiayia's Bread (p. 164) or pita (p. 169) and an herb-infused goat cheese.

3 tbsp olive oil

1 medium onion, finely chopped

3 garlic cloves, minced

1 cup chopped celery

2 cups finely sliced leeks

4 medium potatoes, diced

2 carrots, sliced

1 green bell pepper, chopped

8 cups vegetable broth

1 large tomato, puréed, or 1 cup fresh tomato sauce (unseasoned)

1 bay leaf

1 tsp dried thyme

1 tbsp sea salt (or to taste)

½ tsp freshly ground black pepper

½ tsp cayenne powder (optional)

⅓ cup orzo pasta

Heat olive oil in a large pot on medium. Add onions, garlic, celery, and leeks and sauté until vegetables are slightly soft, about 15–20 minutes. Add potatoes, carrots, green pepper, and broth and bring to a boil. Add tomato sauce, herbs and spices, and orzo pasta. Reduce heat to medium-low and simmer for about 1 hour.

Makes 4–6 servings.

PSAROSOUPA (Fish Chowder)

This is my husband's favorite meal. He grew up in Piraeus, a port just outside of Athens, so his first love is the sea; his second, seafood. When the girls were younger, he would take them on fishing trips and make soup with the day's catch. Traditionally, psarosoupa is made with the whole fish, head and all—if you do, you'll have to remove the bones once the fish is cooked. A truly hearty and healthy dish.

½ cup olive oil
2 large onions, quartered
4 stalks of celery, thickly sliced
4 medium potatoes, cut in eighths
4 carrots, thickly sliced
½ cup chopped fresh parsley
2–3 lbs (1–1.4 kg) fresh cod (scaled and cleaned if using whole fish)
1 tsp sea salt
1 tsp freshly ground black pepper
1 bay leaf
½ cup uncooked white rice (optional)
lemon wedges (1 for each bowl)
freshly ground black pepper, to taste (garnish)

Add olive oil, onions, celery, potatoes, carrots, and parsley to a large pot. Sauté until onions are translucent and the vegetables tender, 15–20 minutes. Add 8 cups of water and bring to a boil. Add fish, salt, pepper, and the bay leaf. Reduce heat to medium-low and simmer for 15–20 minutes.

Once vegetables and fish have cooked, remove from pot. If a whole fish was used, remove the bones once cooked. Add rice, if using, and simmer in stock until cooked, about 20–30 minutes. Add vegetables and fish back to pot once rice has cooked.

Serve each bowl with a lemon wedge and a twist or two of freshly ground black pepper.

Makes 4–6 servings.

SEARED SCALLOP & SPOT PRAWN GAZPACHO

Chef Robert Clark, C Restaurant, Vancouver, BC

Fresh seafood and heirloom tomatoes make this dish a perfect starter to any dinner party. Serve cold to beat the summer heat!

Gazpacho:
2 large red bell peppers, seeds removed, roughly chopped
⅓ medium English cucumber, seeded, peeled, and roughly chopped
2 garlic cloves, halved, with centers removed
¾ cup diced cippolini (or pearl) onions
3 cups fresh heirloom tomato purée
⅓ cup olive oil
⅓ cup red wine vinegar
¾ cup fresh bread cubes (any type of bread)
sea salt, to taste
freshly ground black pepper, to taste
2 tsp Tabasco sauce

Scallops and Prawns:
18 whole spot prawn tails
sea salt, to taste
6 large scallops
2 tbsp olive oil

The day before: Mix the chopped peppers, cucumber, garlic, and onions in a non-reactive mixing bowl, cover, and refrigerate overnight.

Continued next page.

Place the chopped vegetables and the remainder of the gazpacho ingredients in a food processor and purée until smooth. Strain, then refrigerate again for 30 minutes.

Bring a pot of water to a boil, adding enough sea salt to make it taste like the ocean. Add the spot prawn tails and immediately remove from the heat. Let the prawns sit for 30–60 minutes, depending on their size, and remove just before they are completely cooked. Cool the prawns over a bowl of ice, then peel them.

Season the scallops with salt at least 10 minutes before cooking. Heat olive oil in a sauté pan on medium heat and sear the scallops on both sides for 2 minutes per side, cooking to medium rare, then remove from heat.

Pour the chilled soup into very cold bowls, garnish with the seafood, drizzle some extra olive oil on top, and serve.

Makes 4 servings.

HEIRLOOM TOMATO GAZPACHO WITH SHRIMP, CHEESE CURD, & BASIL

Chef Ronald St Pierre, Locals Restaurant, Courtenay, BC

A lovely tomato soup with fresh herbs and olive oil. When tomatoes are in season, head down to your local market and look for varieties of heirloom tomatoes—their taste and colors are simply divine.

2 lb (1 kg) heirloom tomatoes
¼ cup olive oil
2–3 tsp sea salt
1 tsp freshly ground black pepper or cayenne pepper
1 bunch fresh basil
4 oz (125 g) cheese curds
sea salt, to taste
⅓ lb (150 g) cooked, peeled, and chopped shrimp

Purée the tomatoes, olive oil, salt, and pepper in a food processor or blender until smooth and emulsified. Strain to remove skins and seeds. Refrigerate for 1 hour.

Pick 4 nice leaves of basil for garnish and set aside. Finely chop ¼ cup of the basil leaves with the cheese curds, and add salt.

To serve, pour 1 cup of gazpacho into each soup plate. Garnish with the cheese curd and basil mixture and top with fresh shrimp and a basil leaf.

Makes 4 servings.

MAYIRITSA (Traditional Easter Soup)

Following Greek Orthodox Holy week and fasting for Lent, Mayiritsa is the first meat dish eaten after the midnight Easter service. It takes some time to prepare, and you'll probably need to visit a good butcher to find the organ meats, but this is slow food at its best. (Be sure to chop all the meat finely, as my mother did.)

1 lamb tripe	8 green onions, finely chopped
Intestines from a spring lamb (optional)	1 cup fresh dill, finely chopped
1 lamb heart	8–10 cups broth
2 lamb kidneys	¼ cup uncooked white rice
1 lamb liver	1 tsp sea salt
2 lamb shanks	1 tsp freshly ground black pepper
3 tbsp butter	2 eggs
2 tbsp olive oil	juice of 2 lemons

Cut open the tripe and intestines and soak overnight in cold water with lemon juice. Scrape the tripe and rinse well. Scald the tripe, intestines, and organ meats before adding to the recipe.

Boil the tripe and lamb shanks in an uncovered pot until tender, about 1–1½ hours, and reserve the reduced broth (about 6–8 cups). Once all meat is cooked, chop finely into ¼-in (1-cm) dice.

Melt the butter in a large pot on medium heat, then add the olive oil. Stir in green onions, dill, and the finely diced meat. Sauté for 10 minutes. Pour in the broth and bring to a boil. Add the rice. Reduce heat to medium-low, and simmer until the rice is cooked and the meat is tender, about 1½–2 hours. Season with salt and pepper. Remove 1 cup of broth and set aside. Add water to dilute broth if needed.

Beat the eggs until frothy in a small mixing bowl, then add the lemon juice (this will help make the eggs thicken.) While stirring the egg mixture, slowly pour in the hot broth. Return the broth-egg mixture to the soup and stir well. Serve hot.

Makes 4–6 servings.

OXTAIL BARLEY SOUP

My mother and grandmother made this delicious, fortifying soup for us when we were children to warm us up in the winter months. Allow the patient magic of slow cooking to create the unique flavor of this soup. Oxtails are available in many butcher shops.

2 lbs (1 kg) oxtail
¼ cup olive oil
1 medium onion, finely chopped
1 cup barley, soaked overnight in 2 cups water
3 stalks celery, finely chopped
1 cup fresh or frozen corn
1 cup fresh or frozen peas
3 carrots, finely chopped
1 cup finely chopped parsley
2 bay leaves
sea salt, to taste
freshly ground black pepper, to taste
10 whole peppercorns
½ tsp dried thyme
½ tsp cayenne pepper (optional)

Place the oxtails and enough water to cover in a large Dutch oven (or 10gal/L pot) on medium heat. Cook until meat is tender, 1–1½ hours.

Remove meat from pot. Reserve stock. (Alternately, first cook the oxtails in a pressure cooker for about half an hour; this will significantly reduce your total cooking time.)

Heat olive oil in a large soup pot, then add onions and oxtails. Brown meat on all sides and let the onions become soft and translucent. Add reserved stock and the remainder of the ingredients.

Reduce heat to medium-low and simmer for another 1–1½ hours, or until the meat is falling off the bone, the stock is thick, and the vegetables are tender.

Makes 4–6 servings.

YOUVARLAKIA (Meatball Soup)

This traditional Greek soup is as hearty as it gets. Use lean organic meat whenever possible.

1–1½ lbs (½–¾ kg) ground lean beef or venison
1 cup finely minced onion
½ cup finely chopped parsley
½ cup uncooked long grain rice
1 egg, lightly beaten
1 tsp sea salt
1 tsp freshly ground black pepper
6 cups chicken stock or water
½ cup celery leaves
1 cup unbleached white all-purpose flour

Lemon Sauce:
1 cup broth (from soup)
2 eggs
juice of 1 lemon

Combine ground meat, onions, parsley, rice, egg, salt, and pepper in a mixing bowl. Knead well, then form into tablespoon-sized meatballs. Dredge in flour and set aside.

Bring the chicken broth (or water) and celery leaves to a boil in a large pot, then add meatballs to the hot broth. Reduce heat to medium-low and simmer until rice is tender and the meat is cooked, 30–45 minutes. Remove 1 cup of hot broth.

For sauce, beat eggs with a whisk in a small mixing bowl until they are fluffy. Add lemon juice and, while continuing to whisk, slowly add in the cup of hot broth. (Whisking will prevent the eggs from curdling.)

Pour this mixture back into the soup pot and stir well. Season each bowl with a twist or two of freshly ground black pepper and serve hot.

Makes 4–6 servings.

Lamb Souvlaki (page 86) with Tzatziki (page 28) and Baked Lemon Potatoes (page 160)

Quail with Olives (page 110)

ARTICHOKE & VEGETABLE STEW

A hearty vegetarian stew that goes well with focaccia (p. 167), salty hard cheese (like kasseri or sharp white Cheddar), and olives.

3 tbsp olive oil
1 bunch green onions, chopped
6 medium potatoes, chopped into 1-in (2.5-cm) pieces
juice of 1 lemon
4 medium carrots, sliced
¼ cup chopped fresh dill
1 tsp sea salt
freshly ground black pepper, to taste
4 fresh (see p. 37) artichoke hearts, cleaned (or use canned)

Heat olive oil in a large pot on medium and stir in the green onions and potatoes. Sauté until onions are translucent, about 5 minutes. Add lemon juice, carrots, dill, salt, pepper, and enough water to cover. Bring to a boil.

Add artichokes, reduce heat to medium-low, and simmer until vegetables are tender and the stock is thick, 45–60 minutes.

Makes 4 servings.

EUROPEAN STEW

A perfect stew on any winter day. Ask your butcher for free-range and hormone-free beef (or lamb or chicken). Vegetarians can omit the meat and still enjoy this stew. Either way, serve with cheese (try a Greek cheese like Kefalotiri or a sharp, aged Cheddar) and some good bread.

¼ cup olive oil
1 lb (½ kg) beef (or lamb, veal, or chicken), cut into 1-in (2.5-cm) cubes
1 onion, chopped
½ cup red wine
8 potatoes, diced
5 carrots, sliced
4 celery stalks, chopped
1 small eggplant, chopped into 1-in (2.5-cm) pieces
sea salt, to taste
freshly ground black pepper, to taste
1 bay leaf
1 tsp dried oregano

Heat olive oil in a large pot on medium. Add meat and sauté until browned, then add onions and sauté until translucent. Stir in wine and the remainder of the vegetables.

Add salt, pepper, bay leaf, oregano, and enough water to cover. Reduce heat to medium-low and simmer for about 1 hour or until stew is thick.

Makes 4–6 servings.

LAMB & FRESH GREEN BEAN STEW

When slow-cooked in this stew, the lamb becomes mouth-wateringly tender! Serve with an oven-warmed baguette or Yiayia's Bread (p. 164).

3 tbsp olive oil
3 lbs (1½ kg) lamb shoulder, cut in 1-in (2.5-cm) cubes
1 large onion, finely chopped
2 garlic cloves, minced
2 cups crushed tomatoes
2 lbs (1 kg) fresh green beans, cleaned and cut in half
sea salt, to taste
freshly ground black pepper, to taste

Heat olive oil in a large pot on medium. Add lamb and sauté until golden browned, then remove from pot. Stir in the onions and garlic and sauté until lightly browned. Return lamb to pot along with tomatoes and 1–1½ cups water.

Bring to a boil, then reduce heat to medium-low and simmer for 30–40 minutes. Add green beans, salt, and pepper and cook for another 30 minutes or until lamb is tender and the sauce is thick.

Makes 4 servings.

STIFATHO (Venison & Pearl Onion) STEW

This dish was a family favorite when I was growing up, and it was also one I made for my family. Stifatho is best when slowly simmered—adding brilliant flavor and ensuring the most tender meat. It can be made with beef, if you don't have access to venison. Serve over rice pilaf (try the pilaf recipe on p. 157).

3 tbsp olive oil
1 medium onion, finely chopped
3 garlic cloves, minced
2 lbs (1 kg) venison stewing meat, cut in 1-in (2.5-cm) cubes
½ cup red wine
2 cups crushed tomatoes
3 lbs (1½ kg) pearl onions
2 bay leaves
1 tbsp sea salt
freshly ground black pepper, to taste

Heat olive oil in a large pot on medium and add onions, garlic, and venison. Sauté until meat is lightly browned, then add the wine. Bring to a boil, then add tomatoes and about 1 cup of water. Stir in pearl onions, bay leaves, salt, and pepper.

Reduce the heat to medium-low and simmer until meat is tender, the sauce is thick, and the pearl onions soft—but still whole. (Be careful when stirring the pot; you want those onions to remain whole.) Season each serving with freshly ground black pepper.

Makes 4–6 servings.

LAMB SOUVLAKI

LAMB CHOPS WITH ARTICHOKES

LAMB CHOPS WITH OKRA

ROASTED LEG OF LAMB

TURKISH KEBABS WITH GARLIC

PAPOU'S FAYI ("Grandpa's Food" Pork Chops)

LAHANODOLMADES (Cabbage Rolls)

BEEF TENDERLOIN SHISH KEBAB

KEFTEDES (Greek Meatballs)

SOUZOUKAKIA (Meatballs in Tomato Sauce)

Meat & Poultry — Main Dishes —

EGGPLANT & VEAL MEATBALLS

PAPOUTSAKIA (Stuffed Eggplants)

MOUSAKA (Eggplant Lasagna)

NOODLE LASAGNA

KOLOKITHAKIA YEMISTA
(Stuffed Zucchini with Lemon Egg Sauce)

PASTITSIO (Beef and Noodle Casserole)

SOFRITO (Steak with Garlic & Wine)

VENISON PEPPER GARLIC ROAST

QUAIL WITH OLIVES

CHICKEN KOKINESTO

WHOLE CHICKEN BAKED IN A PUMPKIN

ROASTED LEMON CHICKEN & POTATOES

LAMB SOUVLAKI

Barbecued or broiled, souvlaki is always a crowd pleaser, Greek or otherwise. Serve with salad, grilled vegetables, and rice, or in a pita wrap. However you serve it, don't forget the tzatziki (p. 28), and be sure to try the accompaniments on p. 35. (Tip: If using wooden skewers to broil the souvlaki, first soak them in water to prevent the exposed tips from burning.)

2 lbs (1 kg) lamb (or chicken or pork), cut in 1-in (2.5-cm) cubes
½ cup wine, white or red
¼ cup olive oil
3–4 garlic cloves, minced
1 tbsp sea salt
1 tsp freshly ground black pepper
2 tbsp dried oregano

Set oven to broil or turn barbecue on to high.

Mix all ingredients in a large mixing bowl. Let marinate for at least 2 hours (best if overnight).

Place 4–5 pieces of meat on each skewer and broil or barbecue, turning so that meat is browned and cooked evenly on all sides, about 7–12 minutes.

Makes about 20 skewers or 6–8 servings.

LAMB CHOPS WITH ARTICHOKES

The secret to this recipe is to slow cook the lamb, so the meat falls off the bone and the artichokes are tender. The flavor combination here is mouth-watering.

½ cup olive oil
6 green onions, finely chopped
2 lbs (1 kg) lamb loin or shoulder chops
1 tsp sea salt
2 tbsp finely chopped fresh dill
6 artichokes, cleaned and quartered (see p. 37) (or use canned)
juice of 2 lemons
2 eggs
freshly ground black pepper, to taste

Heat olive oil in a deep saucepan on medium. Add green onions and sauté until translucent. Lightly brown lamb chops on both sides, then add enough water to cover, add salt and dill, and bring to a boil. Stir in artichokes and half the lemon juice.

Reduce heat to medium-low and let simmer until meat is tender and the artichokes are cooked, about 45–60 minutes. Remove pan from heat.

Remove 1 cup of broth and set aside. Whisk the eggs in a bowl until foamy. While whisking, slowly add remaining lemon juice to eggs. Continue to whisk, and slowly pour the broth into the egg-lemon mixture. Stir this sauce into the lamb and artichokes. Season the chops with freshly ground black pepper and serve in a shallow bowl with thick slices of fresh crusty bread to mop up the delicious sauce.

Makes 4–6 servings.

LAMB CHOPS WITH OKRA

Okra, the green vegetable that is popular in the American south, is well-loved by Greeks, and is found in cuisines throughout the Mediterranean and Middle East. It is often cooked with acidic foods such as tomatoes, as here, which helps reduce the "sliminess" of the fruits. Serve on a bed of rice or orzo.

¼ cup olive oil
1 bunch green onions, chopped
3 garlic cloves, minced
2 lbs (1 kg) lamb shoulder chops
2 lbs (1 kg) fresh okra, cleaned (or use frozen)
2 cups crushed tomatoes
1 tsp sea salt
freshly ground black pepper, to taste

Heat olive oil in a large saucepan on medium-high. Add onions, garlic, and lamb and sauté until meat is browned.

Remove lamb from pot. Add okra and cook until bright green, about 2–3 minutes. Stir in tomatoes and return lamb to pot. (If too thick, add a little water.)

Reduce to medium and simmer until lamb is tender and the sauce is thick, 45–60 minutes. Season with salt and pepper.

Makes 4–6 servings.

ROASTED LEG OF LAMB

On a spit, in a stew, or roasted in the oven, lamb is loved by all Greeks. Remember to season the meat well. Serve this classic with a green salad and a dry, full-bodied red wine.

3–5 lb (1.5–2.5 kg) leg of lamb
4–6 garlic cloves, slivered
3–4 sprigs fresh rosemary
3 tbsp olive oil
juice of 3 lemons
sea salt, to taste
freshly ground black pepper, to taste
1 tbsp dried oregano
10–15 whole baby potatoes
2–3 carrots, sliced
2 yams, cut in eighths (optional)
3 tbsp olive oil
sea salt, to taste

Preheat oven to 350°F (180°C).

Make small cuts all over the surface of the leg of lamb and insert garlic slivers. Arrange rosemary sprigs in a large roasting pan, and place the lamb on top of the sprigs in the pan. Rub with olive oil, lemon juice, salt, pepper, and oregano. Add about 1 cup water to pan.

Mix potatoes, carrots, yams (if using), olive oil, and sea salt in a large mixing bowl, then add vegetables to the pan. (Add more water if needed, to about 1-in/2.5-cm depth.)

Cover with aluminum foil and roast for 3 hours. Two hours into cooking, remove foil to let lamb brown. Serve hot.

Makes 4–6 servings.

TURKISH KEBABS WITH GARLIC

Izmir-inspired kebabs with garlic offer a true taste of the Orient. Serve with the suggested side dishes (onions, tomato, home-fries) on p. 35 and a dish of full-fat Greek-style yogurt, available in most Mediterranean delis. (If using wooden skewers, soak them in water before broiling to prevent the exposed tips from burning.)

2 lbs (1 kg) ground veal
¼–½ cup lamb fat (available from a butcher)
2 medium onions, minced
3 garlic cloves, minced
sea salt, to taste
freshly ground black pepper, to taste
½ cup chopped fresh parsley
¼ cup olive oil

Set oven to broil.

Knead ground veal, lamb fat, onions, garlic, salt, pepper, and parsley. Form into 2-in (5-cm) long patties and slide onto skewers.

Brush the skewered meat with olive oil and place on an oiled baking sheet. Broil on each side for 7–12 minutes or until browned.

Makes 15–20 skewers or 4–6 servings.

PAPOU'S FAYI ("Grandpa's Food" Pork Chops)

This recipe has been in my family for generations: it was my grandmother Anastasia's special recipe and my grandfather's favorite meal; he loved that the meat was so tender. Hence, it became known in our family as Papou's fayi (or Grandpa's food). This recipe is traditionally made in a clay baker, but a deep pot or covered casserole dish will do.

⅓ cup olive oil
8 pork chops (with fat trimmed) (or venison or veal)
8 onions, finely chopped
3–4 garlic cloves, finely minced
2 tbsp oregano
sea salt, to taste
freshly ground black pepper, to taste
1 cup wine, red or white

Preheat oven to 375°F (190°C).

Heat olive oil in a large frying pan on medium and sauté pork chops until browned on both sides.

Combine the onions, garlic, oregano, salt, and pepper in a mixing bowl. Place a layer of chops in the bottom of a clay baker or deep casserole then cover with the onion mixture. Continue layering chops and onion mixture until all ingredients are used.

Pour in the wine and about 1 cup of water, cover and bake for 1–1½ hours, until the meat is tender and almost falling off the bone. (If you aren't using a clay baker and have a stovetop-safe casserole, you can make this without using the oven.)

Makes 4–6 servings.

LAHANODOLMADES (Cabbage Rolls)

These cabbage rolls can also be made without meat; just add more vegetables and rice instead of ground pork or beef.

1 large green cabbage
½ cup olive oil
1 bunch green onions, finely chopped
1 lb (½ kg) ground pork or beef
1 cup finely chopped green or red bell pepper
1 hot pepper (banana or habañero, but any hot pepper will do),
  finely chopped (optional)
½ cup finely chopped celery (including leaves)
½ cup finely chopped parsley
1 cup crushed tomatoes
1½ cups uncooked white rice
1½ tbsp sea salt
1½ tsp freshly ground black pepper

Preheat oven to 350°F (180°C).

Remove core and outer leaves of cabbage and discard. Bring a large pot of water to a boil. Add cabbage leaves to boiling water a few at a time and blanch for 5–8 minutes, or until tender. Remove cooked leaves from pot to drain and set aside.

Heat olive oil in a large saucepan on medium. Stir in green onions and ground meat and sauté until meat has browned and the onions softened. Add peppers, celery, and parsley. Sauté for a few more minutes, then stir in the tomatoes, rice, salt, and pepper and just enough water to cover. Bring to a boil and reduce heat to low. Cook for 10 minutes or until mixture is thick and not runny. Remove from heat and let cool until it can be handled.

Place 1 tbsp of filling in the center of each cabbage leaf. Fold the left side of the leaf over the mixture, then the right. Now tightly roll the leaf from bottom to top, making sure no filling spills out. If desired, secure each leaf with a toothpick. Continue until all mixture is used.

Arrange the cabbage rolls in a 9 x 12-in (23 x 30-cm) baking pan. Add enough water to cover. Bake for 1 hour or until rice is cooked.

Makes 6 servings.

BEEF TENDERLOIN SHISH KEBAB

Serve with Greek Salad (p. 58) and Sage Rice Pilaf (p. 157). You can also use chicken or lamb instead of beef. If using wooden skewers, soak them in water before broiling to prevent the exposed tips from burning.

2 lbs (1 kg) beef tenderloin (or round steak), cut into 1½-in (3.75-cm) cubes
4 medium onions, cut into quarters
2 green bell peppers, seeded and cut into eighths
4 tomatoes, cut into eighths
10–15 button mushrooms (optional), cut in half
1 large zucchini (optional), cut in 1½-in (3.75-cm) pieces
1 large eggplant (optional), cut in 1½-in (3.75-cm) pieces
juice of 2 lemons
1 cup dry red wine
¼ cup olive oil
1 tbsp sea salt
1 tsp freshly ground black pepper
1 tsp rose pepper
1 tbsp chopped fresh rosemary
6 garlic cloves, minced

Preheat barbecue, or set oven to broil.

In a large bowl, combine all ingredients and let marinate in the refrigerator overnight (or for 3–4 hours).

Skewer the meat and vegetables alternately, leaving 1 in (2.5 cm) uncovered on both ends of the skewer. Place skewers on the barbeque or on a lightly oiled baking sheet, browning them on both sides, about 10 minutes.

Makes 4–6 servings.

KEFTEDES (Greek Meatballs)

My kids love these meatballs. Make them bite-sized and they are a perfect snack.
Add a green salad and a glass of wine and you have a tasty quick meal.

1½ lb (¾ kg) lean ground beef
1 cup white or whole wheat bread cubes, soaked in water
2 large onions, grated or finely diced
3 garlic cloves, minced
2 eggs
2 tbsp fresh (or dried) mint
1 tbsp dried oregano
1 tsp freshly ground black pepper
sea salt, to taste
about 1½ cups flour, seasoned to taste with sea salt, pepper, and garlic powder
¼–½ cup olive oil

Combine all ingredients, except for flour and olive oil, in a mixing bowl and knead together well. Marinate for 2–3 hours in the refrigerator. Form into 1-in (2.5-cm) balls and roll in seasoned flour. Dust off any excess flour.

Heat olive oil in a large frying pan on medium-high. Add meatballs and fry until golden brown and cooked through, 5–8 minutes each side.

The keftedes may alternately be cooked under the broiler in a pan. If using this method, there is no need to dredge them in flour. Simply roll in olive oil and place on a baking sheet. Broil until golden brown and cooked through, 5–8 minutes each side. Serve hot or cold.

Makes 4–6 servings.

SOUZOUKAKIA (Meatballs in Tomato Sauce)

My mother made the best souzoukakia, garlic and cumin-rich, and a perfect blend of Greek and Turkish culinary styles. They're wonderful on their own, tossed in pasta, or between thick slices of French bread.

Souzoukakia:
2 lbs (1 kg) lean ground beef
2 eggs
1 cup breadcrumbs
1 tbsp dried oregano
1 tbsp dried basil
1 tbsp cumin
6 garlic cloves, minced
1 large onion, grated
1 cup wine, red or white
1 tsp sea salt
1 tsp freshly ground black pepper
about 1 cup flour
2–4 tbsp olive oil

Tomato Sauce:
4 tbsp olive oil
3 garlic cloves, minced
4 cups crushed tomatoes (fresh or canned)
½ cup dry red wine
½ tsp dried thyme
sea salt, to taste

Combine all souzoukakia ingredients (except for the flour and olive oi)l in a large mixing bowl. Refrigerate for 2–3 hours.

Remove from fridge and roll mixture into small oval (1½-in/4-cm) meatballs, then dredge meatballs in flour. Heat olive oil in a large frying pan on medium-high and fry souzoukakia until golden brown and cooked through. Remove from heat and prepare the tomato sauce as follows.

For the tomato sauce, heat olive oil in a large saucepan on medium. Add garlic and sauté until fragrant, then stir in the remainder of the ingredients. Reduce heat to medium-low and simmer for 30 minutes. Add the prepared meatballs to the sauce and continue to simmer until sauce is thick, 45–60 minutes. Serve on their own or over linguine or spaghetti.

Makes 6–8 servings.

EGGPLANT & VEAL MEATBALLS

Serve over your favorite pasta. For a vegetarian meal, use 1 large grated zucchini and a 1-lb (454-g) package of tofu instead of the meat.

1 large eggplant
1 lb (½ kg) ground veal
1–2 garlic cloves, minced
1 cup breadcrumbs
2 onions, finely chopped
1 tsp dried oregano
1 egg
½ cup chopped fresh parsley
sea salt, to taste
freshly ground black pepper, to taste
2 cups tomato sauce (p. 96)
½–¾ cup mozzarella cheese, grated

Preheat oven to 400°F (205°C).

Place the eggplant on a lightly oiled baking sheet and bake whole for 30–45 minutes, or until soft. Reduce oven temperature to 350°F (180°C).

Let eggplant sit until cool enough to handle. Peel the skin off the eggplant and discard. Squeeze any excess liquid from the flesh, then mash it well with a fork or potato masher.

Combine the eggplant, veal, garlic, breadcrumbs, onions, oregano, egg, parsley, salt, and pepper and knead together until well-mixed. Form mixture into 1-in (2.5-cm) meatballs and place side-by-side in a lightly oiled 9 x 12-in (23 x 30-cm) baking pan. Cook meatballs under the broiler until browned, about 5–7 minutes. Cover with tomato sauce, sprinkle with cheese, and cover pan with aluminum foil and bake for 10–15 minutes. Bake for 30–45 minutes covered, then remove foil and bake for 10–15 minutes.
Serve over pasta of your choice.

Makes 4–6 servings.

PAPOUTSAKIA (Stuffed Eggplants)

Papoutsakia means "little shoes." Think of these as a mini lasagna in an eggplant casing. You can make this vegetarian by omitting the meat.

8 small eggplants, 5–6-in each (13–15-cm)
2 fresh tomatoes, finely chopped
½ cup finely chopped fresh parsley
½ cup olive oil
1 cup ground beef or venison
1 small onion, finely minced
½ tsp sea salt
½ tsp freshly ground black pepper

Béchamel Sauce:
¼ cup olive oil (or butter)
½ cup unbleached white flour
2 cups milk, at room temperature
1 egg, beaten
sea salt, to taste
freshly ground black pepper, to taste
½ tsp nutmeg

Topping:
3–4 tbsp grated Parmesan or Kefalotiri cheese
3–4 tbsp unsalted butter

Set oven to broil.

Remove stems from and cut the eggplants in half, lengthwise. Hollow them out using a spoon. Combine the eggplant flesh, tomatoes, and parsley in a blender.

Salt the insides of the eggplant casings and squeeze out any excess water. Brush casings with olive oil and place on a baking sheet. Broil until lightly browned and slightly soft.

Heat olive oil in a saucepan on medium, then stir in meat and brown. Add onions and half the tomato mixture and sauté until the sauce is thick, 20–30 minutes. Season with salt and pepper and remove from heat.

To make the béchamel: heat olive oil (or butter) in a small saucepan on medium-low. Slowly whisk in the flour and then the milk, and continue whisking until the mixture is smooth. Beat the egg in a small mixing bowl, then add to the milk mixture, continuing to stir and making sure the egg doesn't harden. Season with salt, pepper, and nutmeg, and continue to stir until the sauce is smooth and thick (about 15–20 minutes).

Preheat oven to 375°F (190°C).

Arrange the eggplant casing in a lightly oiled 9 x 12-in (23 x 30-cm) baking pan. Fill each casing with the meat mixture and top with the béchamel sauce. Sprinkle tops of each eggplant with cheese and dabs of butter. Add the rest of the blended eggplant-tomato mixture and 1 cup of water to the pan and bake for 45 minutes or until brown.

Makes 4–6 servings (16 papoutsakia).

MOUSAKA (Eggplant Lasagna)

A Greek take on the classic lasagna. Vegetarians can opt for thin slices of potatoes instead of ground beef. Top with slices of Kefalotiri, a flavorful Greek cheese made with sheep's milk. (Kefalotiri can be purchased at most Mediterranean delis.)

sea salt, to taste
4 large eggplants, peeled and sliced into 1-in (2.5-cm) pieces
1 tbsp olive oil
¼ cup olive oil
1½ lb (¾ kg) lean ground beef (or lamb)
1 large onion, chopped
½ cup finely chopped parsley
1 cup crushed tomatoes (fresh or canned)
1 tsp sea salt
½ tsp freshly ground black pepper
½ cup breadcrumbs

Béchamel Sauce:
¼ cup olive oil (or butter)
⅔ cup unbleached white flour
3 cups milk, room temperature
2 eggs
sea salt, to taste
freshly ground black pepper, to taste
½ tsp nutmeg

Topping:
½ cup grated Kefalotiri cheese

Set oven to broil.

Salt eggplant slices on both sides and arrange them on a lightly oiled cookie sheet. Brush each slice, on both sides, with olive oil, using a pastry brush. Place the sheet under the broiler and bake for 3–5 minutes on each side, until golden brown.

Heat olive oil in a medium saucepan on medium. Stir in the ground meat and onions and sauté until meat has browned and the onions are soft. Add parsley, tomatoes, salt, and pepper and simmer until liquid is reduced, about 30 minutes. Mix in breadcrumbs and remove from heat.

Brush a 9 x 12-in (23 x 30-cm) baking pan with olive oil and line bottom of pan with eggplant slices. Cover with one layer of the meat mixture, then continue alternating eggplant and meat layers until all ingredients are used.

To make the béchamel: heat olive oil (or butter) in a small saucepan on medium-low. Slowly whisk in the flour and then the milk, and continue whisking until the mixture is smooth. Beat the eggs in a small mixing bowl, then add to the milk mixture, continuing to stir and making sure the egg doesn't harden. Season with salt, pepper, and nutmeg, and continue to stir until the sauce is thick (about 15–20 minutes).

Preheat oven to 375°F (190°C).

Pour béchamel over the eggplant and meat layers in the baking pan. Sprinkle with grated cheese and bake for 1 hour or until top has browned.

Makes 6–8 servings.

NOODLE LASAGNA

A classic. Want to add more veggies? Try a layer of spinach leaves or grated zucchini (with its juices squeezed out first, so it doesn't make the dish too watery). Simmer your sauce for as long as you can: slow cooking means more flavor.

Meat Sauce:
½ cup olive oil
1 medium onion, finely chopped
2 garlic cloves, minced
1 lb (½ kg) lean ground beef (or venison)
½ cup red wine
2 cups crushed tomatoes (fresh or canned)
1 tsp dried oregano
sea salt, to taste
freshly ground black pepper, to taste

Cheese Mixture:
2 cups ricotta cheese
½ cup grated Parmesan cheese
2 eggs

9-oz (225-g) package of lasagna noodles, cooked
 (you may not need to use the whole package)
1 cup grated mozzarella cheese

Preheat oven to 350°F (180°C).

Heat olive oil in a large saucepan on medium. Stir in the onions and garlic and sauté until onions are soft. Add ground meat and let brown, then pour in wine and bring to a boil. Add the tomatoes, oregano, salt, pepper, and about 1 cup of water. Reduce heat to medium-low and simmer for 1 hour.

Mix ricotta and Parmesan cheeses, and eggs in a bowl.

Spread a thin layer of meat sauce in the bottom of a lightly oiled 9 x 12-in (23 x 30-cm) baking dish. Lay down a single layer lasagna noodles over the sauce and cover with a layer of cheese mixture. Alternate between the noodles, meat sauce, and cheese mixture until all ingredients are used.

Top off with mozzarella cheese and cover with aluminum foil. Bake for 45 minutes. Remove foil and bake for another 10–15 minutes or until lightly browned.

Makes 4–6 servings.

KOLOKITHAKIA YEMISTA
(Stuffed Zucchini with Lemon Egg Sauce)

Basil and I grow zucchinis in our garden, in part because we both love Kolokithakia Yemista. This traditional Greek meal can also be made without the ground meat for a hearty vegetarian option. The tangy Lemon Egg Sauce is essential, however!

3 lbs (1½ kg) whole zucchinis, approx. 6-in (15-cm) long

1 lb (½ kg) lean ground beef

½ cup uncooked long-grain rice

½ cup olive oil

2 large onions, finely chopped

½ cup finely chopped fresh mint

½ cup finely chopped fresh parsley

1 fresh tomato, grated

1 tbsp sea salt

1 tsp freshly ground black pepper

Lemon Egg Sauce (recipe following)

Preheat oven to 350°F (180°C).

Cut the tops off the zucchinis and hollow them out using a spoon. Reserve 1½ cups of the zucchini flesh and the zucchini tops. Salt the hollowed-out zucchini lightly.

Brown the ground beef in a small frying pan on medium.

Finely chop the reserved zucchini flesh, then combine with browned ground beef, rice, half the olive oil, onions, mint, parsley, tomato, salt, and pepper in a mixing bowl. Knead the mixture well. Stuff each zucchini casing with the filling, to about ½-in (1-cm) from the top (leaving room for the rice to expand when cooked).

Now place the tops on each filled casing, secure with a toothpick if needed, and arrange in a large baking pan. Add 1 in (2.5 cm) of water and the remainder of the olive oil. Bake for approximately 1 hour. Reserve 3 cups of pan juices. Serve topped with Lemon Egg Sauce.

Makes 4 servings.

Lemon Egg Sauce:
3 tbsp olive oil
3 tbsp flour
3 cups pan juices from stuffed zucchini
sea salt, to taste
2 eggs
juice of 2 lemons

Heat the olive oil in a saucepan on low, and slowly add in the flour while constantly stirring, until it becomes a smooth paste. Slowly mix in all but 1–2 tbsp of the pan juices, add salt, and simmer, stirring frequently, for 2–5 minutes.

Beat eggs until creamy in a mixing bowl, then stir in lemon juice. Add 1 or 2 tbsp of the pan juices to the egg mixture, being careful not to let the eggs curdle. Slowly add the egg mixture to the rest of the stock, and stir well (do not let sauce come to a boil). When the sauce has thickened, about 3–5 minutes, remove from heat. Pour sauce over baked stuffed zucchinis.

Makes 4–4½ cups.

PASTITSIO (Beef & Noodle Casserole)

No tavern in Greece would be without it, but nothing beats homemade pastitsio! This dish is creamy, filling, and delicious.

¼ cup olive oil

1½ lb (¾ kg) lean ground beef

2 onions, finely chopped

1 tsp sea salt

½ tsp freshly ground black pepper

1–2 bay leaves

2 cups crushed tomatoes (fresh or canned)

1 lb (½ kg) ziti macaroni

2 cups grated Parmesan or Kefalotiri cheese

Béchamel Sauce:

½ cup melted, olive oil (or butter)

1½ cups flour

6 cups milk, warm

2 eggs

sea salt, to taste

freshly ground black pepper, to taste

1 tsp nutmeg

Preheat oven to 375°F (190°C).

Heat olive oil in a medium saucepan on medium-high and then stir in beef and onions. Sauté until the meat has browned and the onions are soft. Mix in salt, pepper, bay leaves, and tomatoes. Reduce to medium heat and simmer for 30–45 minutes.

Bring a large pot of water to a boil, add macaroni, and cook for 10 minutes or until tender. Rinse with cold water and drain well. Pour cooked macaroni, 1½ cups of the grated cheese, beaten eggs, milk, and butter into a mixing bowl and combine.

To make the béchamel: heat olive oil (or butter) in a small saucepan on medium-low. Slowly whisk in the flour and then the milk, and continue whisking until the mixture is smooth.

Beat the eggs in a small mixing bowl, then add to the milk mixture, continuing to stir and making sure the eggs don't harden. Season with salt, pepper, and nutmeg, and continue to stir until the sauce is thick (about 15–20 minutes).

In a lightly oiled 9 x 13-in (23 x 33-cm) baking pan, arrange ⅓ of the macaroni. Spread ⅓ of the meat sauce over the pasta, and continue to layer macaroni and meat sauce until all has been used. Top off with béchamel sauce and the remaining ½ cup of cheese. Cover with foil and bake for 40–45 minutes. Remove foil and bake for 10–15 minutes or until the sauce has set and the top of the pastitsio is golden brown.

Makes 6–8 servings.

SOFRITO (Steak with Garlic & Wine)

Sofrito is a traditional recipe from the island of Corfu in the Ionian Sea. Makes a great accompaniment to skordalia (garlic mashed potatoes p. 159).

2 veal cutlets (traditionally made with veal, but you can use beef or venison escalopes)
sea salt, to taste
freshly ground black pepper, to taste
½ cup flour
¼ cup butter
8 garlic cloves, minced
¼ cup olive oil
½ cup wine, red or white

Rub salt and pepper into both sides of the steaks, then dredge in flour.

Melt the butter in a large frying pan on medium and add the steaks. Brown on both sides. Remove the steaks from the pan and add the garlic to the pan. Sauté for just a minute, until fragrant, then stir in the olive oil and wine.

Return steaks to the pan and reduce heat to low. Simmer until the meat is tender. Season with more salt and/or pepper if desired.

Makes 2 servings.

VENISON PEPPER GARLIC ROAST

Venison will dry out easily unless handled properly, so be sure to thoroughly rub the roast with olive oil and season it well before it goes in the oven. (Boneless beef rib or leg of lamb roast may be substituted if you don't have venison.)

6 garlic cloves, slivered
3 lbs (1½ kg) venison roast
2 tbsp olive oil
1 tbsp sea salt
1 tbsp freshly ground black pepper
2 tsp dried thyme
½ cup wine, red or white
4 medium potatoes, quartered (and/or carrots, parsnips, or yams) (optional)

Preheat oven to 375°F (190°C).

Make small cuts all over the surface of the roast and insert garlic slivers. Brush the roast with olive oil and rub well with salt, pepper, and thyme. Pour about 1 cup water and the wine into a baking pan big enough to hold the roast (and root vegetables, if you're using).

Place the roast in the pan and cover with foil. (If using vegetables, season them first with olive oil and salt and pepper, then add to pan 1 hour into baking time.)

After 1½ hours, remove foil to let the roast bake until tender, about 10 minutes. Remove from oven, strain pan juices, and use as *au jus* or base for gravy.

Makes 4–6 servings.

QUAIL WITH OLIVES

My mother cooked many game dishes; my father was a hunter. Who knew my husband would one day take up this sport too? This recipe is my personal favorite. The flavor from the olives, rosemary, and quail meat go perfectly with a simple green salad, orzo or wild rice, and a nice glass of white wine. Cheers!

6 quail (or other small game birds), cut in half

2 cups wine, red or white (for marinating)

½ cup olive oil

4 garlic cloves, finely chopped

4 sprigs fresh rosemary

1 tbsp dried oregano

1½ cups sundried or green olives (rinse to remove excess saltiness)

2 cups crushed tomatoes (fresh or canned)

1 cup wine

1 tsp sea salt, or to taste

1 tsp freshly ground black pepper

In a deep glass baking pan, immerse the halved quails in wine and marinate for a few hours or overnight, turning occasionally.

Heat olive oil in a large pot on medium, then add quail and brown on all sides. Stir in the garlic, rosemary, oregano, olives, crushed tomatoes, wine, salt, pepper, and enough water to half cover the quail.

Cover the pot and simmer on low heat until meat is tender, 30–45 minutes. (Alternately, transfer to a baking pan and cook at 350°F [180°C] for 2 hours, or until the meat is tender and the sauce is thick.)

Makes 4–6 servings.

CHICKEN KOKINESTO

This Greek dish of chicken with crushed tomatoes is slow food at its best. Cook at low heat until meat is tender. Serve on orzo pasta and sprinkle with Parmesan cheese. Kokinesto can also be prepared with rabbit, veal, or lamb.

3 tbsp olive oil
1 medium whole chicken, cut in serving pieces
2 garlic cloves, minced
1 medium onion, finely chopped
2 cups finely chopped celery
½ cup olive oil
½ cup wine, red or white
2 cups crushed tomatoes (fresh or canned)
1 tsp sea salt
½ tsp freshly ground black pepper
1 bay leaf
2 cups orzo pasta, cooked
½ cup grated Parmesan cheese

Heat olive oil in a large saucepan on medium and brown the chicken pieces. Remove chicken from pan and drain off excess fat. Stir in garlic, onions, and celery and sauté until onions are translucent.

Return the chicken to the pan along with ½ cup olive oil, wine, tomatoes, 1–2 cups water, salt, pepper, and bay leaf. Bring to a boil, then reduce heat and simmer for 1½ hours, or until the sauce is thick and the chicken is tender and falling off the bone. Remove from heat. Serve over pasta and garnish with Parmesan cheese.

Makes 4–6 servings.

WHOLE CHICKEN BAKED IN A PUMPKIN

Chef Vincent Stufano, Fairmont Chateau Whistler, Whistler, BC

A whole chicken roasted inside a pumpkin! Be sure to save the pumpkin flesh after you remove the chicken—this makes an amazing, savory soup base. Choose a free-range, organically raised chicken for this recipe. (Vegetarians can use root vegetables instead of chicken.)

1 pumpkin (large enough to hold
  a whole chicken)
6 tbsp olive oil
1 tsp cinnamon
1 tsp allspice
sea salt, to taste

freshly ground black pepper, to taste
20 fresh sage leaves
10 fresh thyme branches
1 3-lb (454 g–1½ kg) chicken
1 cup sliced porcini mushrooms

Preheat oven to 375°F (190°C).

Cut off the top of the pumpkin to form a 5-in (13-cm) lid. Scoop out the seeds and stringy bits. Rub the inside of the pumpkin with half the olive oil, half the cinnamon and allspice, and season with salt and pepper, as desired. Place a handful of sage and fresh thyme in the bottom of the pumpkin.

Rub the chicken with remaining olive oil, cinnamon, and allspice and season with salt and pepper. Now place the chicken inside the pumpkin. Stuff the porcini mushrooms on top of the chicken along with a branch of thyme and handful of sage leaves. Place the lid back on the pumpkin and bake for approximately 3 hours, or until chicken is cooked and pumpkin flesh is soft.

Remove pumpkin from the oven and let rest for ½ hour. Remove the lid, cut the pumpkin in half horizontally, and gently lift out the chicken.

Scoop out the pumpkin flesh and reserve for the best pumpkin soup you've ever had.

Makes 4–6 servings.

ROASTED LEMON CHICKEN & POTATOES

This dish is all about the lemons, which help to tenderize the meat and add great flavor to the potatoes!

1 chicken, cut in quarters
1 tsp sea salt
1 tsp pepper
1 tsp thyme, dried or fresh
1 tsp rosemary, dried or fresh
½ tsp cayenne pepper
2 garlic cloves, minced
2 whole lemons, quartered
¼ cup olive oil
4 medium potatoes, quartered
2 carrots, sliced on a bias (optional)

Preheat oven to 375°F (190°C).

Rub chicken pieces with salt and pepper and cover with thyme, rosemary, cayenne pepper, and garlic. Squeeze juice from 1 lemon (reserve rind) and combine with olive oil in a large, non-reactive baking pan. Place chicken in the pan to marinate in the refrigerator, covered, overnight.

Add 1–2 cups of water, potatoes, carrots, juice from the second lemon, and all the squeezed-out lemon rinds to the pan. Bake for 1–1½ hours, or until potatoes are tender and the meat golden brown. Remove lemon rinds before serving.

Makes 4 servings.

BAKED COD

BAKED LING COD WITH TOMATO-CAPER FONDUE
AND SMOKED EGGPLANT PURÉE

SOLE AU NATUREL

SOLE WITH GARLIC & PEPPERCORNS

SABLEFISH WITH PRESERVED LEMONS & CAPER SAUCE

GARLIC BREADED SNAPPER

SNAPPER À LA MÉDITERRANÉE

BARBECUED WILD SALMON

SALMON & SEAFOOD PASTA

Fish & Seafood
— Main Dishes —

OLIVE OIL-POACHED SALMON WITH FETA VINAIGRETTE

BARBECUED OYSTERS

GARIDES YOUVETSI ME FETA (Shrimp with Feta)

LEMON GARLIC SHRIMP

OCTOPUS IN WINE SAUCE

KALAMARIA YEMISTA (Stuffed Squid)

CALAMARI WITH ONIONS & WINE

FRIED CALAMARI

BAKED COD

A simple and tasty recipe that my mother taught me. Try it on the barbecue (wrapped in foil) for a smoky flavor.

1 lb (½ kg) cod fillets (4 pieces)
1 tsp sea salt
2 tomatoes, finely chopped
1 medium onion, finely chopped
1 cup finely chopped parsley
2 garlic cloves, minced
1 tsp sea salt
½ tsp freshly ground pepper
½ cup olive oil

Preheat oven to 350°F (180°C) or prepare barbecue.

Salt fish and set aside. Combine tomatoes, onions, parsley, garlic, salt, pepper, and olive oil in a mixing bowl.

Line a baking pan with aluminum foil. Cover with tomato mixture, then place fish on top. Cover with foil and bake for 25–30 minutes in the oven, or 15–20 minutes on a barbecue on medium heat.

Makes 4 servings.

BAKED LING COD WITH TOMATO-CAPER FONDUE AND SMOKED EGGPLANT PURÉE

Frank Pabst, Blue Water Cafe, Vancouver, BC

Unmistakable Mediterranean flavors are layered to enhance the delicious rich taste of ling cod.

8 large Roma tomatoes
½ cup extra virgin olive oil
3 garlic cloves, finely chopped
2 shallots, finely diced
zest of 1 lemon
5 basil leaves, 3 of them
  chiffonaded (shredded)
1 tbsp capers, rinsed and chopped
8 Italian parsley leaves, chiffonaded
pinch of espelette pepper
  (or substitute hot paprika)
1 large Italian eggplant
¼ onion, chopped

½ jalapeño pepper, seeded
  and chopped
1 sprig thyme
dash of red wine vinegar
½ lemon
4 tbsp panko breadcrumbs
4 fillets of ling cod, ⅓ lb (150 g)
  each, skin and pinbones removed
salt, to taste
freshly ground black pepper, to taste
pinch of fennel pollen
  (or coarsely ground fennel seeds)

Bring a large pot of water to a boil. Add tomatoes and blanch for 30 seconds, then plunge them into an ice bath. Peel and seed the tomatoes, then finely dice the flesh.

In a medium sauté pan, heat 4 tbsp of the olive oil on medium heat. Add 1 garlic clove and sauté until it becomes fragrant and just begins to brown, then add shallots. Cook for 30 seconds longer and add tomatoes, lemon zest, and the 2 whole basil leaves. Cook over low heat for about 30 minutes, stirring regularly, until all of the tomato water has evaporated and the fondue starts to thicken. Add capers and Italian parsley and season with salt and espelette pepper. Remove from heat, allow to cool, then refrigerate.

Continued next page.

Preheat a barbecue or grill. Grill eggplant whole, with the barbecue's lid down, until all sides are well charred and a smoky flavor develops. The eggplant should be very soft to the touch.

In a medium pot, heat 2 tbsp of the olive oil on medium heat. Add onion, jalapeño, thyme, and the remaining 2 cloves of garlic and cook for 5–10 minutes until fragrant and lightly browned.

Cut the cooked eggplant in half, scoop out the flesh, and add it to the onion mix. Continue to cook the eggplant mix until all liquid has evaporated, about 10 minutes, then remove the thyme and add red wine vinegar.

Blend this mixture in a food processor with 3 tbsp of your best extra virgin olive oil, then strain the purée through a sieve (use a plastic-mesh sieve to avoid oxidation). Add shredded basil and adjust seasoning with salt and pepper and a squeeze of lemon juice.

In a small bowl, toss together panko breadcrumbs and 1 tbsp of olive oil.

Preheat the oven to 425° F (220°C).

Place cod in a lightly oiled baking pan. Season cod fillets with salt, pepper, and fennel pollen. Cover each fillet with a layer of the tomato fondue, then top with a thin layer of panko breadcrumbs. Bake for 12–15 minutes, or until the fish is just done and the crust is golden. To serve, spread one large spoonful of eggplant purée in the center of each of four plates. Top with a ling cod fillet and finish the dish with a drizzle of extra virgin olive oil.

Makes 4 servings.

SOLE AU NATUREL

Sole is a delicious light and flaky fish, high in omega fats and taste!

2 lbs (1 kg) sole fillets
2 tbsp finely chopped parsley
1 tbsp olive oil
juice of 1 lemon
sea salt, to taste
1 lemon, quartered

Preheat oven to 350°F (180°C).

Season the sole with dill, olive oil, lemon juice, and salt and place in a baking pan. Bake for 10–15 minutes, or until fish is cooked. Serve with lemon wedges to squeeze over the fish.

Makes 4 servings.

SOLE WITH GARLIC & PEPPERCORNS

This recipe calls for "rose" peppercorns, which aren't peppercorns at all but berries of the Baies rose. They add a sweet, fruity, and slightly spicy flavor to the delicate sole.

2 lbs (1 kg) sole fillets
sea salt, to taste
10 garlic cloves, crushed into a fine paste
3 tbsp olive oil
juice of 1 lemon
1 tsp sea salt
½ tsp freshly ground black pepper
3 tbsp rose peppercorns, ground
½ tsp cayenne pepper
1 tsp dried thyme

Lightly season fish with salt and place in an oiled baking pan. Combine remainder of ingredients in a small bowl, then spread over fish. Cover and refrigerate for 2 hours.

Preheat oven to 350°F (180°C).

Bake for 10–15 minutes, or until fish is flaky and white.

Makes 4 servings.

SABLEFISH WITH PRESERVED LEMONS & CAPER SAUCE

Chef Lynda Larouche, (formerly at) Watermark Restaurant, Vancouver, BC

Sablefish is a sleek, black-skinned fish from the cold, deep waters of the North Pacific. Also known as black cod or butterfish, sablefish is commonly available smoked but is becoming increasingly obtainable unsmoked. It's prized for its pearly white flesh and large velvety flakes. Rich in oil, sablefish is equally good fresh or frozen. Note: Make the preserved lemons a week before you plan to serve this dish.

1 lemon quarter from preserved lemon mixture, prepared 1 week earlier
  (see following)
4 oz (115 g) capers (large ones are best)
1 cup olive oil
4–5oz (115–140g) sablefish fillets, with skins on
2–3 tbsp olive oil
sea salt, to taste
cracked white pepper, to taste

Preheat oven to 350°F (180°C).

Finely dice a preserved lemon quarter, then combine with capers and the olive oil in a small bowl.

Pat the fillets dry, and heat olive oil in a large frying pan to the almost-smoking stage. Season the fish with salt and pepper and place into the frying pan. Sear the skinless side first to obtain a great blond color.

Flip the fish over and finish in the oven for 15 minutes. Pour the lemon-caper mixture over the fish and serve with your favorite starch and vegetables.

Makes 4 servings.

Continued next page.

Preserved Lemons:
5 lemons, cut into quarters
¼ cup sea salt
1 cinnamon stick
3 garlic cloves
5–6 coriander seeds
4 black peppercorns
1 bay leaf
¼ cup sugar

Mix all ingredients well in a large bowl. Place into a 2-pint (or 750-mL) jar and let sit for 1 week at room temperature. (Once opened, the preserve needs to be refrigerated, where it will keep for up to three months.)

GARLIC BREADED SNAPPER

Serve with steamed greens such as kale or Swiss chard or with a green salad and homemade fries (p. 35).

1 lb (½ kg) snapper fillets
1 tbsp olive oil
sea salt, to taste
4 garlic cloves, grated or crushed
½ cup bread crumbs
sea salt, to taste
freshly ground black pepper, to taste
¼ cup olive oil
1 whole lemon, quartered

Brush fillets with olive oil, salt well, and spread with garlic.

Combine the breadcrumbs with salt and pepper. Dip fillets into seasoned bread-crumbs and set aside for 1 hour.

Heat olive oil in a frying pan on high and fry fillets until golden brown (a few minutes on either side). Serve with fresh lemon wedges.

Makes 4 servings.

SNAPPER À LA MÉDITERRANÉE

*Simple and elegant, you can serve with skordalia (p. 159), steamed greens
(p. 138), and Latholemono Sauce (see below).*

sea salt, to taste
2 lbs (½ kg) snapper fillets (or salmon steaks)
3 tbsp olive oil
1 tsp dried oregano
freshly ground black pepper or pinch of cayenne pepper (optional)
Latholemono Sauce (see recipe below)

Preheat oven to 375°F (190°C).

Salt snapper fillets well, then brush with olive oil and rub with oregano and pepper.
Marinate for 1 hour in the fridge.

Bake snapper until flesh becomes opaque, about 3–5 minutes on each side,
depending on the thickness of the fillet; don't overcook the fish or it will dry out.
Place the cooked snapper on a platter and drizzle with the sauce.

Makes 2–4 servings.

Latholemono (Lemon and Oregano) Sauce:
This sauce is a Greek staple. Use on grilled fish and vegetables and steamed
greens (p. 138), too.

juice of 2 lemons
½ cup olive oil
½ tsp sea salt
freshly ground black pepper, to taste
2 tsp dried oregano

Beat all ingredients in a small mixing bowl until emulsified. Pour over cooked fish.

Makes 1 cup.

BARBECUED WILD SALMON

Wild salmon is your best choice! This is great served with a green salad with thinly sliced red and yellow bell peppers tossed in a honey, Dijon mustard, lemon juice, and olive oil dressing, sprinkled with whole pomegranate seeds.

5 lbs (2½ kg) whole wild salmon (sockeye or spring are best)
sea salt, to taste
freshly ground black pepper, to taste
2 tsp garlic powder or 1 tbsp finely minced fresh garlic
1 tbsp dried oregano
1 whole lemon, sliced into ¼-in (6-mm) rounds
Latholemono Sauce (see p. 124)

Prepare barbecue.

Season fish (inside and out) with salt and pepper. Rub entire fish with garlic (powdered or fresh) and oregano. Line the inside of fish with lemon slices.

Place fish on lightly oiled barbecue, and cook for 15–20 minutes on each side. Once cooked, remove from heat. Carefully remove the skin and drizzle the sauce over the fish.

Makes 4–6 servings.

SALMON & SEAFOOD PASTA

Simple enough to make on a weeknight, delicious enough to serve to guests.

3 tbsp olive oil
1 onion, finely chopped
2 garlic cloves, minced
½ cup finely chopped green bell pepper
6 cups fresh tomato sauce (p. 96) or canned, crushed tomatoes
sea salt, to taste
freshly ground black pepper, to taste
½ cup fresh basil
1 tbsp fresh oregano
1 lb (½ kg) wild salmon, cut in 2-in (5-cm) cubes
½ lb (¼ kg) shrimp, peeled and deveined
1 cup fresh or canned clams, cleaned
pasta shells, cooked (enough for 4–6 people)
¼–½ cup grated Parmesan cheese

Heat olive oil in a medium saucepan on medium. Add onions, garlic, and green pepper and sauté until tender. Add tomato sauce or tomatoes and bring to a boil, then add salt, pepper, oregano, and basil.

Reduce heat to medium-low and simmer for 30 minutes or until sauce is thick. Add seafood and simmer for 20–30 minutes, or until cooked. Serve over pasta shells and garnish with grated Parmesan cheese.

Makes 4–6 servings.

OLIVE OIL-POACHED SALMON WITH FETA VINAIGRETTE

Chef Christophe Kwiatkowsky, Northwest Culinary Academy of Vancouver, Vancouver, BC

A great fusion of tangy and savory. Serve with salad and steamed Yukon gold nugget potatoes.

1 qt/L olive oil
2–4 tbsp dried oregano
4 6-oz (170-g) wild salmon fillets, 1-in (2.5-cm) thick, skin on (sockeye or spring
  salmon are best)

Feta Vinaigrette:
2 roma tomatoes, diced
½ cup crumbled feta cheese
12 olives, any kind
1 tbsp Corinthian currants (or raisins)
2 tbsp balsamic vinegar
¼ cup olive oil
sea salt, to taste
freshly ground black pepper, to taste
¼ cup sugar

Continued next page.

Combine all vinaigrette ingredients in a bowl and set aside.

Heat olive oil in a deep-sided saucepan to a temperature of 265°F (130°C). Turn the heat off, place the oregano into the oil, and allow to infuse for 30 minutes. Strain.

Reheat the oil to 175°F (80°C) (poaching temperature). Place the 4 salmon fillets into the oil and allow to poach for approximately 15 minutes with the flesh down at a consistent temperature of 175°F (80°C). Cook fish until the internal temperature reaches 140°F (60°C), which will ensure the salmon is moist and slightly under-cooked.

Heat a cast-iron skillet and sear the salmon, skin-side down only. Remove from heat. Slice each fillet in half on a bias and present with one half skin-side up and one half skin-side down. Spoon the feta vinaigrette over the salmon.

Makes 4 servings.

BARBECUED OYSTERS

When our daughters were little, they loved to go oyster hunting—although it took them years to appreciate the taste of the oysters themselves. Buy oysters as fresh as you can get them. Serve with crusty bread and chilled white wine.

½ cup olive oil
6–8 garlic cloves, minced
juice of 4 lemons
cayenne pepper, to taste
sea salt, to taste
36 oysters, shucked (retain shells for serving)

Preheat barbecue to high.

Heat olive oil in a small pot on medium. Add garlic and lemon juice and bring to a boil. Add cayenne pepper and salt. Remove from heat.

When you have shucked the oysters, choose the side of the shell that has a deeper well and place the oyster in it. Pour a little prepared sauce on each oyster and place shell on the barbecue. Let the oyster and sauce come to a boil. When oyster is firm (1–2 minutes), remove from heat.

Makes 6–8 servings.

GARIDES YOUVETSI ME FETA (Shrimp with Feta)

In Greece, this dish is traditionally made in clay pots, but you can use a casserole dish or Dutch oven. Serve as a main course over a bed of rice with a green salad or steamed vegetables on the side.

1½ lbs (¾ kg) shrimp, peeled and deveined
juice of ½ lemon
3 tbsp olive oil
½ cup finely chopped onion
3 garlic cloves, finely minced
4 green onions (green part only), finely chopped (or chives)
1 cup crushed tomatoes (fresh or canned)
½ cup dry white wine
1 tsp dried oregano
2 tbsp finely chopped parsley
sea salt, to taste
freshly ground black pepper, to taste
1–1¼ cups feta cheese, crumbled or cubed

Preheat oven to 400°F (205°C).

Place shrimp in a bowl and squeeze lemon juice on shrimp. Heat ½ the olive oil in a frying pan on medium-high, add shrimp, and cook until shrimp has turned pink. Remove from heat and set aside. Add the rest of the olive oil to the pan and heat on medium-high. Add onions and garlic and sauté until lightly golden brown. Add green onions, tomato, wine, oregano, parsley, salt, and pepper. Reduce heat to medium and simmer for 15 minutes. Remove from heat.

Pour tomato sauce and shrimp into a casserole and top with feta cheese. Bake for 20 minutes, or until hot and bubbly.

Makes 4–6 servings.

LEMON GARLIC SHRIMP

On the barbecue or under the broiler, shrimp with lemon and garlic is a Koutalianos family favorite. Serve over a bed of rice.

½ cup olive oil
3 garlic cloves, minced
24 large shrimp, shells removed with tails left on
½ cup chopped parsley
1 tsp dried oregano
juice of 2 lemons
sea salt, to taste
freshly ground black pepper, to taste
½ cup water or vegetable broth

Heat olive oil in a medium saucepan on medium. Add garlic and shrimp and sauté, then add remaining ingredients and bring to a boil for 5 minutes.

Makes 4–6 servings.

OCTOPUS IN WINE SAUCE

My husband and daughter Anastasia adore this dish. Make sure the octopus is cleaned well (remove and discard the octopus's tiny beak and ink sack) and boil until tender.

1 tsp sea salt
2 lbs (1 kg) octopus, cleaned and left whole
¼ cup olive oil
½ cup wine, red or white
¼ cup wine vinegar
1 tsp sea salt
1 tsp dried oregano

Bring a large pot of salted water to a boil. Add whole octopus and cook until tender, approximately 1–1½ hours, depending on size. Remove 1 cup of broth from pot and set aside. (Alternatively, you can cook the whole octopus in the oven. Season with salt and oregano, and bake at 450°F (230°C) for 1½ hours, or until the octopus is tender.)

Remove octopus from pot or oven and cut into 1-in (2.5-cm) pieces. Add octopus, olive oil, wine, vinegar, salt, and reserved broth (or 1 cup water) and let simmer until sauce thickens, 45–60 minutes.

Remove from heat, arrange octopus pieces on a platter and sprinkle with oregano and a dash of vinegar, if desired, and let cool. Serve chilled or at room temperature.

Makes 4–6 servings.

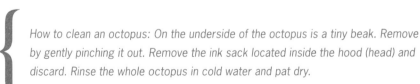

How to clean an octopus: On the underside of the octopus is a tiny beak. Remove by gently pinching it out. Remove the ink sack located inside the hood (head) and discard. Rinse the whole octopus in cold water and pat dry.

KALAMARIA YEMISTA (Stuffed Squid)

Stuffed calamari is one of Basil's favorites. Serve this dish with an asparagus or dill bean salad (p. 51 or p. 56).

2 lbs (1 kg) squid, cleaned and left whole
2 large fresh tomatoes, finely chopped
6 green onions, finely chopped
½ cup chopped parsley
½ cup olive oil
¾ cup uncooked long-grain rice
2 tsp sea salt
½ tsp freshly ground black pepper

Preheat oven to 375°F (190°C).

Combine the tomatoes, green onions, parsley, olive oil, rice, sea salt, and pepper in a mixing bowl. Mix well. Using a small spoon, stuff the mixture into the squid's pouch. (Any leftover stuffing can be used to cover the calamari in the pan.)

Lay the squid in a shallow 9 x 12-in (23 x 30-cm) baking pan and add enough water to just cover. Cover dish with aluminum foil and bake for 45 minutes.

Remove foil and continue to bake uncovered for 15 minutes.

Makes 4–6 servings.

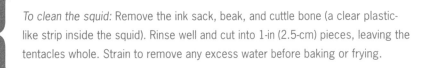

To clean the squid: Remove the ink sack, beak, and cuttle bone (a clear plastic-like strip inside the squid). Rinse well and cut into 1-in (2.5-cm) pieces, leaving the tentacles whole. Strain to remove any excess water before baking or frying.

CALAMARI WITH ONIONS & WINE

This simple and tasty dish is one of my grandmother's best recipes. The onions add sweetness and help thicken the wine sauce. Serve over rice. You'll lick your fingers!

½ cup olive oil

10 medium onions (yellow, white, or red), finely chopped

3 lbs (1½ kg) squid, cleaned (see p. 133) and cut into 1-in (2.5-cm) pieces

1 cup red wine

2 tsp sea salt, to taste

1 tsp freshly ground black pepper

½ tsp cayenne pepper

Heat olive oil in a large saucepan on medium. Add onions and sauté until translucent. Add squid and continue to sauté until it turns slightly pink, 5–7 minutes. Add wine and bring to a boil. Add salt, black pepper, cayenne pepper, and just enough water to cover.

Reduce heat and simmer for 1 hour or until the calamari is tender and the sauce is thick.

Makes 4–6 servings.

FRIED CALAMARI

As Greek as feta cheese, calamari is a fantastic appetizer or a main course, served with rice and salad. Not a fan of fried foods? Drizzle with olive oil and bake instead. Whatever your preference, serve with plenty of tzatziki (p. 28) or garlic aioli (p. 25).

1 tsp sea salt
2 lb (1 kg) calamari, cleaned (see p. 133) and cut into 1-in (2.5-cm) pieces
1 cup flour
sea salt, to taste
freshly ground black pepper, to taste
cayenne pepper, to taste
garlic powder, to taste
1 cup olive oil (or, if using deep fryer, up to 3 cups)
juice of 1 lemon
1 onion, finely chopped (garnish)
½ cup finely chopped fresh parsley (garnish)

Salt calamari and set aside. In a bowl, combine flour, salt, pepper, cayenne, and garlic powder and dredge calamari pieces in mixture.

Heat olive oil in a frying pan (or deep-fryer) on medium-high. Add calamari and fry until golden brown, 3–5 minutes. Remove from pan and set on a paper towel for a moment to absorb any excess oil.

Place on a serving dish, drizzle with lemon juice, and garnish with onions and parsley. Serve hot.

Makes 2–4 servings.

SEASONAL GREENS WITH LEMON & OLIVE OIL

AGINARES LEMONATES (Artichoke Stew with Lemon)

ARTICHOKE PARMESAN

KAPAKOTO (Roasted Eggplant & Pepper Casserole)

IMAM BAYILDI (Stuffed Baby Eggplants)

EGGPLANT PARMESAN

MELITZANA KSIPOLITI (Eggplant Quiche)

OKRA IN ANGEL HAIR PASTA

POTATO FRITTATA

TOMATO FRITTATA

GIGANDES (Giant Baked Lima Beans)

FAVA (split Yellow Peas)

Vegetarian Main
— & Side Dishes —

REVITHOKEFTEDES (Chickpea Patties)

TIROPITA (Cheese & Phyllo Pie)

SPANAKOPITA (Spinach & Cheese Pastry)

LEEKS IN PHYLLO

DOLMADES (Rice Wrapped in Grape Leaves)

DOMATES YEMISTES (Rice-Stuffed Tomatoes)

SAGE RICE PILAF OR STUFFING

SAUERKRAUT & RICE CABBAGE ROLLS

SKORDALIA (Garlic Mashed Potatoes)

BAKED LEMON POTATOES

FASOLAKIA YAHNI (Green Bean & Potato Stew)

BRIAM (Roasted Root Vegetables)

SEASONAL GREENS WITH LEMON & OLIVE OIL

Greens are very important in the Greek diet. Dandelion greens and nettles (known as sesoula and vlita) are much sought after. (Too bad the dandelion is considered a weed in North America; it is packed with nutrients.) Whether you forage for wild greens in the springtime or go to your local farmer's market for kale, spinach, or Swiss chard in the summer and fall, each season brings us different greens, reminding us to eat what is in season. This recipe shows that simple and unadorned foods are also delicious and good for us.

1–2 large bunches of fresh seasonal greens, rinsed well
¼ cup olive oil
juice of 1 lemon
sea salt, to taste

In a pot of water with a steamer, lightly steam greens until tender but not wilted and strain. Place steamed greens in a bowl and gently toss with olive oil, lemon juice, and sea salt. Serve warm or cold.

Makes 4 servings.

AGINARES LEMONATES (Artichoke Stew with Lemon)

Fresh dill and artichokes make this dish. Remove the artichokes' stiff outer leaves and use only their tender hearts … your guests will love you! Makes a great side dish for lamb chops (p. 87).

½ cup olive oil
8 green onions, finely chopped
4 medium artichokes, cleaned (see p. 37)
4 potatoes, cut into 2-in (5-cm) cubes
3 carrots, sliced in rounds
juice of 2 lemons
¼ cup finely chopped fresh dill
sea salt, to taste
freshly ground black pepper, to taste
1 tbsp flour (optional)

Heat olive oil in a large saucepan on medium. Add green onions and sauté for 2–3 minutes, then stir in artichokes, potatoes, and carrots. Pour in enough water to cover, add lemon juice, dill, salt, and pepper.

Cook for ½ hour. Remove ½ cup of liquid from the pot and place in a small bowl. Add flour and mix until smooth (no lumps). Add flour mixture back into the pot and stir until combined well. Continue cooking for ½ hour or until artichokes are tender.

Makes 4 servings.

ARTICHOKE PARMESAN

The perfect marriage of fresh and savory.

2 medium artichokes, cleaned (see p. 37) and cut into quarters
sea salt, to taste
freshly ground black pepper, to taste
1 egg, beaten
½ cup grated Parmesan cheese
½ cup flour
2–3 tbsp olive oil
3 tbsp coarsely chopped fresh dill (garnish)
1 lemon, quartered (garnish)

Salt and pepper the artichokes. Place the beaten egg, Parmesan cheese, and flour in separate bowls. Dip the artichokes in the egg, then cheese, then flour, until well-coated. Shake off excess flour.

Heat olive oil in a medium saucepan on medium-high, and sauté artichokes until leaves are tender and golden brown, 3–5 minutes on each side. Serve hot or at room temperature with a sprinkle of fresh dill and lemon wedges.

Makes 2 servings.

KAPAKOTO (Roasted Eggplant & Pepper Casserole)

I first sampled Kapakoto, an eggplant dish layered with feta cheese, on a recent trip to Greece. Serve hot or at room temperature as a side dish for souvlaki (p. 86) with a simple green salad.

2 medium eggplants, cut in 1-in (2.5-cm) thick slices
4 bell peppers (any color), seeded and quartered
3 tbsp olive oil
3–4 garlic cloves, finely chopped
2 tbsp fresh or dried oregano
2 cups crumbled feta cheese
1 cup breadcrumbs
2–3 fresh tomatoes, cut into ½-in (1-cm) thick slices
1 onion, finely minced (optional)
sea salt, to taste
freshly ground black pepper, to taste
2–3 tbsp olive oil

Set oven to broil.

Brush eggplant slices and peppers on both sides with olive oil and place on a baking sheet. Broil on each side for 2–5 minutes or until brown.

Reset oven temperature to 375°F (190°C). In a lightly oiled 9 x 12-in (23 x 30-cm) baking pan, arrange a layer of the grilled eggplant slices. Sprinkle evenly with ⅓ of the garlic, oregano, cheese, and breadcrumbs. Top with a layer of grilled peppers and repeat layer of garlic, oregano, cheese, and breadcrumbs.

Arrange the final layer of eggplant, top with tomato slices and onions, then season with pepper and salt and the remainder of the garlic, oregano, cheese, and breadcrumbs.

Drizzle with olive oil. Bake for about 1 hour or until top is lightly browned.

Makes 4–6 servings.

IMAM BAYILDI (Stuffed Baby Eggplants)

A dish my mother made when I was young, Imam Bayildi is a fusion of Turkish and Greek cuisines.

8 small (about 4-in/10-cm long) eggplants
sea salt, to taste
3 large fresh tomatoes, finely chopped
3 medium onions, finely chopped
3 garlic cloves, minced
1 cup finely chopped fresh parsley
sea salt to taste
freshly ground black pepper, to taste
1 cup olive oil
juice of 1 lemon
1 large tomato, sliced
salt, to taste
freshly ground black pepper, to taste

Preheat oven to 375°F (190°C).

Remove stems from the eggplants. Make three slits lengthwise in each eggplant and sprinkle with sea salt. Let sit on baking sheet or cutting board for 30 minutes. Squeeze out any excess liquid from the eggplants and set aside.

Combine the finely chopped tomatoes, onions, garlic, parsley, salt, pepper, olive oil, and lemon juice in a mixing bowl.

Stuff filling into slits in eggplants. Arrange the stuffed eggplants in a large baking pan and cover with sliced tomato. (Add any leftover filling to the pan.) Salt and pepper the tomatoes and add about 1 cup of water to pan. Cover the pan with aluminum foil and bake for 1 hour, or until the eggplants are soft. Serve hot or cold.

Makes 4–6 servings.

EGGPLANT PARMESAN

Eggplants are a staple in the Mediterranean diet. These make a great appetizer, served hot or at room temperature.

3 tbsp olive oil
2 garlic cloves
1 cup crushed tomatoes (fresh or canned)
1 tsp sea salt
½ tsp freshly ground black pepper
sprig of fresh basil
2 medium eggplants, cut into ½-in (1-cm) slices
1 tsp sea salt
2–3 tbsp olive oil
1 cup grated mozzarella cheese
½ cup grated Parmesan cheese

Heat olive oil in a medium saucepan on medium. Add garlic and sauté until fragrant, then add tomatoes, about ½ cup water, salt, pepper, and basil. Reduce heat to low and simmer for 30–45 minutes.

Meanwhile, salt eggplant slices on both sides and arrange on a lightly oiled baking sheet. Let sit for 30 minutes. Squeeze out any excess liquid.

Set oven to broil. Brush eggplant slices with olive oil and broil for 2–5 minutes on each side, or until golden brown.

Set oven to 375°F (190°C). Arrange one layer of the grilled eggplant slices in a 9 x 12-in (23 x 30-cm) casserole dish and cover with part of the tomato sauce. Alternate until all ingredients are used, finishing with the sauce. Sprinkle with mozzarella and Parmesan cheeses and bake for 45 minutes, or until lightly browned.

Makes 4–6 servings.

MELITZANA KSIPOLITI (Eggplant Quiche)

A Mediterranean twist on quiche, without the pastry. Fresh herbs and flavorful Greek cheeses make this dish unique. Don't go for seconds, though—it tastes even better the next day! Japanese eggplants are smaller than the more common variety, with a thinner skin; you could also use small regular eggplants.

4 Japanese eggplants
3 tbsp olive oil
4 medium onions, finely chopped
4 eggs
1 cup grated Kefalotiri cheese
1 cup crumbled feta cheese
½ cup chopped fresh dill
½ cup chopped fresh fennel greens
½ cup fresh chopped mint
½ cup uncooked long-grain rice
sea salt, to taste (you don't need much as the cheeses are both quite salty)
1 tsp freshly ground black pepper
1 cup breadcrumbs
1 tbsp olive oil

Aginares Lemonates (page 139)

Tahini Koulouria (page 184) and
Almond Biscotti (page 181)

Preheat oven to 375°F (190°C).

Make several random slits in the skin of each eggplant. Bake the eggplants on a baking sheet for 30–45 minutes.

Remove and discard eggplant skins. Cut the cooked flesh into 1-in (2.5-cm) pieces, lightly salt, and set aside.

Heat olive oil in a small saucepan on medium. Add the onions and cubed eggplants, and sauté until the onions are translucent. Remove from heat.

Beat the eggs in a mixing bowl, then stir in the cheeses, dill, fennel greens, mint, rice, sautéed onions and eggplants, salt, and pepper. Mix well.

Place half the breadcrumbs in a well-oiled quiche pan, pour in the eggplant mixture, and sprinkle the top with the remainder of breadcrumbs. Drizzle with olive oil and bake for 45 minutes until golden. Serve warm or at room temperature.

Makes 4 servings.

OKRA IN ANGEL HAIR PASTA

A Koutalianos family favorite (and one of mine, too, as it can be made in minutes).
Top off with a garnish of Parmesan or Kefalotiri, a Greek cheese made from
sheep's milk.

¼ cup olive oil
3 garlic cloves, minced
4 cups okra, tops cut off
3 medium tomatoes, puréed
sea salt, to taste
freshly ground black pepper, to taste
angel hair pasta, cooked (enough for 4 people)
½–1 cup grated Parmesan or Kefalotiri cheese

Heat olive oil in a saucepan on medium. Add garlic and sauté until light brown, then add okra. Cook until the okra turns bright green (about 5 minutes).

Lower heat to medium-low. Add puréed tomatoes, salt, and pepper. Simmer for 30–45 minutes. Serve over angel hair pasta and top with the cheese.

Makes 4 servings.

POTATO FRITTATA

This was my mother's quick-lunch fix just before restocking the pantry and fridge. It also makes a hearty addition to any breakfast or brunch. Best with real potatoes; forget those frozen imposters!

½ cup olive oil
3 medium potatoes, any kind, cut into ¾-in (2-cm) cubes
6 eggs, lightly beaten
sea salt, to taste
freshly ground black pepper, to taste
¼–½ cup grated Parmesan cheese

Preheat oven to 375°F (190°C) Heat olive oil in a large frying pan on medium-high. Add potatoes, and fry until golden brown and slightly soft, about 15–20 minutes. Remove potatoes from pan and set aside.

Combine eggs, salt, pepper, and 1 tbsp water and beat until fluffy. Pour the eggs into the frying pan that was used to cook the potatoes. Stir potatoes into the egg mixture and cook on medium heat for 5–10 minutes (or until the fritatta is cooked and golden in color).

Using a plate to cover the frying pan, flip the frittata and then cook on the other side for about 4–5 minutes. Sprinkle with Parmesan cheese before serving.

Alternately, the frittata can be finished in the oven. Oil a 9 x 12-in/23 x 30-cm baking pan, then pour in the eggs and fried potatoes. Top with cheese and bake until cooked thoroughly and browned on top (about 30–45 minutes). There is no need to turn the frittata if cooked in the oven.

Makes 2–4 servings.

TOMATO FRITTATA

Nothing says summer more than a fresh tomato frittata. You can't go wrong with this recipe: just make sure the tomato is well-cooked and any excess liquid has evaporated before adding to the eggs.

3–4 tbsp olive oil
1 garlic clove, minced
1 medium onion, finely chopped
2 large tomatoes, finely chopped
sea salt to taste
freshly ground black pepper, to taste
6 eggs, beaten
½ cup crumbled feta

Preheat oven to 375°F (190°C).

Heat olive oil in a small saucepan on high. Add garlic, onion, and tomatoes. Sauté until tomatoes have softened and most of the liquid has evaporated. Season with salt and pepper.

Pour vegetable mixture and eggs into a lightly oiled 9 x 12-in (23 x 30-cm) baking pan, top with feta, and bake until cooked thoroughly for 30–45 minutes.

Makes 4 servings.

GIGANDES (Giant Baked Lima Beans)

Gigandes is traditionally served as a picantico (side dish). These baked beans are slowly simmered to bring out the most intoxicating of aromas and flavors. Patience is key and well-rewarded. Great with a fine glass of wine, a sharp cheese, and a loaf of crusty bread.

2 cups large lima beans, cooked (see below) or canned
2 cups crushed tomatoes (fresh or canned)
½ cup olive oil
2 large onions, finely chopped
1 cup finely chopped chives
3 garlic cloves, minced
1 cup finely chopped parsley
1 tbsp sea salt
1 tsp freshly ground black pepper
cayenne pepper, to taste

Preheat oven to 375°F (190°C).

Place cooked lima beans in a lightly oiled 9 x 12-in (23 x 30-in) baking pan. Stir in tomatoes, olive oil, onions, chives, garlic, and parsley. Add salt, black pepper, and cayenne pepper. Add enough water to cover and bake for 1–2 hours, or until beans are completely soft and the sauce is thick.

Makes 4–6 servings.

{ *How to prepare the lima beans:* Soak beans in water overnight, then drain water. Bring 2 qt/L fresh water to a boil in a large pot. Add beans and reduce to medium heat. Simmer for 1–1½ hours (beans should be tender but not mushy). Remove from heat and drain.

FAVA (Split Yellow Peas)

This dish was once considered peasant food. Now, fava is being served in some of the finest restaurants in Greece. Regardless of its newfound prestige, fava is reminiscent of a time long gone, when mothers made all food from scratch.

2 cups split yellow peas, washed and strained
1 large cooking onion, cut in quarters
1 tsp sea salt

Garnish:
1 cup finely chopped fresh parsley
½ cup finely chopped red onion
juice of 1 lemon
sea salt, to taste
1–3 tbsp olive oil

Bring 4 cups water to a boil in a large pot. Add yellow peas, onions, and salt. Bring back to a boil for 5–10 minutes, then reduce heat. Simmer until peas and onions are soft and the mixture is thick, about 1 hour. (While the beans are cooking, discard any foam that surfaces in the pot.)

Purée beans in a blender or with a hand blender until smooth. Pour into a shallow serving dish and let cool. Top with the various garnishes and serve chilled or at room temperature. (As the fava cools, it will thicken.)

Makes 4–6 servings.

REVITHOKEFTEDES (Chickpea Patties)

A great snack or lunch for vegetarians. Serve with green salad or wrap them in pita bread (p. 169) with hummus (p. 26) or tzatziki (p. 28), like a falafel.

2–3 cups cooked (or canned) chickpeas (garbanzo beans)

2 tsp finely chopped garlic

1 tbsp powdered cumin

1 tbsp dried mint

1 tsp dried oregano

½ cup finely chopped fresh parsley

1 cup breadcrumbs

1 tsp sea salt

1 tsp freshly ground black pepper

1 egg, lightly beaten

1 cup flour, seasoned with salt and pepper, to taste

about ½ cup olive oil

Purée cooked or canned chickpeas in a blender or food processor until smooth. Combine puréed chickpeas, garlic, cumin, mint, oregano, parsley, breadcrumbs, salt, pepper, and egg in a mixing bowl. Knead mixture into a soft dough. Form into small patties and dredge in seasoned flour.

Heat olive oil in a large frying pan and fry patties on each side for 3–5 minutes, or until golden brown.

Makes 10–15 patties.

TIROPITA (Cheese & Phyllo Pie)

If you've ever been to Greece, chances are you've had a tiropita. Made with delicate phyllo pastry and tasty feta cheese, tiropitas are a delicious finger food.

1–1½ cups feta cheese, crumbled
2 eggs, lightly beaten
sea salt, to taste (taste the feta for saltiness before adding any salt)
freshly ground black pepper, to taste
1 1-lb/454-g pkg phyllo pastry
2–3 tbsp olive oil

Preheat oven to 375°F (190°C).

Combine feta cheese, eggs, and seasoning in a mixing bowl.

Cut phyllo pastry into strips about 3 inches wide using a sharp knife. Pull off 2 layers of phyllo pastry at a time and lightly brush with olive oil. Keep unused phyllo under a moist towel to prevent it from drying out.

Place about 1 tbsp of cheese mixture at bottom of each 2-layer strip of phyllo. Fold phyllo at an angle over the mixture from right to left (to form a triangle). Next, fold this triangle up to the right. Continue folding phyllo at angles, keeping the mixture tucked in, until you've reached the top of the strip and a neat triangle shape is formed. Brush top of triangle with olive oil. Repeat until all the cheese mixture has been used.

Place on an oiled baking sheet and bake for 40 minutes, or until golden brown.

Makes about 30 pies.

SPANAKOPITA (Spinach & Cheese Pastry)

Spanakopita is a staple in any Greek home and one my daughter Vicki makes well.
Great as a snack or a side.

2 bunches spinach, washed, dried, and roughly chopped
½ cup finely chopped fennel, bulb and greens
6 green onions, finely chopped
sea salt, to taste (taste the feta for saltiness before adding salt)
freshly ground black pepper, to taste
1 cup crumbled feta cheese
4 eggs, lightly beaten
2 tbsp uncooked white rice
¼ cup olive oil
1 1-lb/454-g pkg phyllo pastry

Preheat oven to 375°F (190°C).

Combine spinach, fennel, green onions, salt, and pepper in a bowl, then mix in
feta, eggs, and rice. Lightly oil a 9 x 12-in (23 x 30-cm) baking pan with olive oil.
Line the bottom of the pan with one phyllo sheet at a time, carefully brushing each
layer with olive oil. Keep unused phyllo under a moist towel to prevent it from drying out. Repeat with 5–6 sheets, then spread the spinach mixture evenly over the
phyllo. Layer another 5–6 sheets of pastry (brushing each sheet with olive oil) onto
the spinach mixture.

Sprinkle a little water on the final sheet to prevent it from cracking before placing
in the oven. Bake for 30–45 minutes, or until golden brown.

Makes 4–6 servings.

LEEKS IN PHYLLO

Basil and I love leeks—our garden is full of them! Wrap them in phyllo and you have a great snack or side dish. Add feta cheese to this recipe, if you like, but if you do, add less salt or omit it entirely.

6 leeks, cleaned and thinly sliced, white part only
¼ cup finely chopped fresh dill
4 eggs, lightly beaten
1 tsp sea salt (optional)
½ cup feta cheese (optional)
½ tsp freshly ground black pepper
1 1-lb/454-g pkg phyllo pastry
¼ cup olive oil

Preheat oven to 400°F (205°C).

Using a pastry brush, lightly oil a 9 x 12-in (23 x 30-cm) baking pan.

Combine the leeks, dill, eggs, salt, and pepper.

Line the bottom of the pan with one phyllo sheet at a time, carefully brushing each layer with olive oil. Keep unused phyllo under a moist towel to prevent it from drying out. Repeat with 5–6 sheets, then spread the leek and egg mixture evenly over the phyllo (if there is excess liquid, drain it off first). Layer another 5–6 sheets of phyllo (brushing each sheet with olive oil) onto the leek mixture.

Sprinkle a little water on the final sheet to prevent it from cracking before placing it in the oven. Bake 30–40 minutes, or until golden brown.

Makes 4–6 servings.

Wash leeks thoroughly, as they often have a lot of grit between the leaves.

DOLMADES (Rice Wrapped in Grape Leaves)

When I was a child, my grandmother would take me out early in the morning to collect grape leaves. She showed me how to select only the tenderest of leaves. Then, when we got home, she'd start to make dolmades. I can still picture her folding each one and carefully placing them in the pot in a perfectly round pattern, topping each layer with a row of single leaves and then more dolmades. This is not a quick recipe; it takes time and patience but is well worth the effort.

1 16-oz/474-mL jar of grape leaves in brine
   (or about 35–50 fresh leaves
   when in season, see sidebar)
3 tsp olive oil
1 bunch green onions, finely chopped
1 fresh tomato, grated (about 1 cup)

3 tbsp chopped fresh mint
   (or 1 tbsp dried)
1 tbsp sea salt
1½ tsp freshly ground pepper
1½ cups long grain rice
1 cup olive oil

If harvesting your own fresh grape leaves, cut leaves without the stem from the grapevine. Avoid picking leaves that have been sprayed with chemicals. Wash them well before using.

Preheat oven to 350°F (180°C).

Remove grape leaves from brine (if not using fresh leaves) and rinse in cold water. Bring a large pot of water to a boil, add grape leaves, and let boil for 1–2 minutes, then drain.

Heat 3 tbsp olive oil in a medium saucepan on medium-low and gently sauté green onions for 8–10 minutes. Stir in tomatoes, mint, salt, pepper, rice, and 1 cup olive oil. Add water to cover and bring to a boil, then reduce heat and let simmer for 5–8 minutes.

Remove from heat. Once mixture has cooled, place 1 tsp of filling in the center of a grape leaf. Fold the bottom of the leaf over the filling. Tuck the left and right sides of the leaf over the filling and roll tightly from the bottom to the top into a cigar shape. Place the folded dolmades, seam sides down, in a 9 x 12-in (23 x 30-cm) baking pan. Add water to the pan until dolmades are just covered, and cook until liquid is absorbed and the rice is cooked, 45–60 minutes. Serve warm or cold with a topping of plain Greek-style yogurt.

Makes 6–8 servings.

DOMATES YEMISTES (Rice-Stuffed Tomatoes)

This is a Greek staple. Use tomatoes when in season. You may also add ground beef to the stuffing for a heartier meal, but whatever you do, don't overcook the rice.

10 large tomatoes
¼ cup finely chopped fresh mint
1 bunch green onions, finely chopped
1 cup olive oil
2 cups uncooked long-grain rice
1 tbsp sea salt
½ tsp freshly ground black pepper
¼ cup grated Parmesan cheese

Preheat oven to 350°F (180°C).

Cut tops off tomatoes to create "lids" and set them aside. Seed and core the tomatoes. Strain seeds from pulp.

Blend the seedless tomato pulp in a food processor until smooth. Reserve ¼ of the pulp and set aside.

Combine remainder of the pulp in a mixing bowl with mint, green onions, olive oil, rice, salt, and pepper and mix well. Stuff mixture into hollowed-out tomatoes until ⅔ full, and cover with tomato lids.

Pour reserved tomato pulp and about 1 cup of water into a 9 x 12-in (23 x 30-cm) baking pan, then place stuffed tomatoes on top. Sprinkle Parmesan cheese over tomatoes. Bake for about 1 hour or until rice is tender. Serve hot or at room temperature.

Makes 4–6 servings.

SAGE RICE PILAF OR STUFFING

My daughter Anastasia loves this dish. It's great on its own or can be used as poultry (chicken, turkey, game birds) stuffing. Add diced roasted chestnuts for a nuttier taste.

¼ cup olive oil
2 tbsp butter
1 medium onion, finely chopped
1 cup finely chopped celery
½ cup raisins (or currants)
½ cup raw pine nuts
1–2 cups uncooked long grain rice
1 tbsp dried sage leaves
1 tsp sea salt
1 tsp freshly ground black pepper
1 chicken or turkey liver, finely chopped (optional)

Heat olive oil and melt butter in a large saucepan on medium-high. Add onions and celery and sauté for 5–8 minutes, or until tender. Stir in raisins, pine nuts, rice, sage, salt, pepper, and liver, if using. Add 1 cup water and reduce heat to medium.

Simmer uncovered for 20–30 minutes, until rice is semi-cooked, if using as poultry stuffing, or continue to cook on stove top for an additional 20–30 minutes, until rice is cooked.

Makes 4–6 servings.

SAUERKRAUT & RICE CABBAGE ROLLS

A tangy twist on the standard cabbage roll. Freeze leftovers for busy days, or make tighter, smaller rolls and serve them as an appetizer.

1 large green cabbage
½ cup olive oil
1 large onion, finely chopped
2 cups sauerkraut (do not drain liquid)
1½ cups uncooked long-grain rice
1 cup crushed tomatoes (fresh or canned)
1 tsp paprika
1 tsp finely chopped dried or fresh mint
1 tbsp sea salt
1 tsp freshly ground black pepper

Preheat oven to 350°F (180°C).

Remove core and outer leaves of cabbage and discard. Bring a large pot of water to a boil. Add cabbage leaves to boiling water a few at a time and blanch for 5–8 minutes, or until tender. Remove blanched leaves from pot and set aside.

Heat olive oil in a large saucepan on medium-high. Add onions and 1 cup of the sauerkraut, and sauté until onions are translucent, about 5–8 minutes. Add rice, tomatoes, paprika, mint, salt, and pepper. Remove from heat and let cool.

Place 1 tbsp of filling on each cabbage leaf. Fold top and bottom edges of leaf over mixture, tuck the sides in, then roll up into a cigar shape. Continue until all mixture and/or cabbage leaves are used. Pour reserved sauerkraut and its liquid in the bottom of a 9 x 12-in (23 x 30-cm) baking pan.

Arrange cabbage rolls in the pan seam side down. Cover pan with aluminum foil and bake for 1 hour, or until rice is tender.

Makes 6 servings.

SKORDALIA (Garlic Mashed Potatoes)

In Greece, skordalia is traditionally served cold or at room temperature. It's great with grilled or fried fish and steamed greens.

8 medium potatoes (any kind), peeled and cut into small cubes
6 garlic cloves, crushed
1 cup olive oil
4 tbsp white vinegar
sea salt, to taste

Bring a large pot of water to a boil. Add potatoes and cook for 15–20 minutes or until tender, then drain. Combine the cooked potatoes with the garlic, olive oil, vinegar, and salt. Blend until smooth in a food processor or in a large mixing bowl using a hand blender.

Chill in fridge for 3–4 hours or overnight before serving.

Makes 6–8 servings.

BAKED LEMON POTATOES

A great accompaniment to any dish. For melt-in-your-mouth lemony potatoes, first partially boil and drain, then combine with other ingredients and let marinate in the refrigerator overnight before baking.

6 medium potatoes (Yukon gold preferred), cut in quarters
juice of 2 lemons
½ tsp dried oregano
½ cup olive oil
sea salt, to taste
freshly ground black pepper, to taste

Preheat oven to 350°F (180°C).

Combine all ingredients in a 9 x 12-in (23 x 30-cm) baking pan. Toss well, then add about 2 cups water to the pan.

Bake for 45–60 minutes, or until golden brown.

Makes 4–6 servings.

FASOLAKIA YAHNI (Green Bean & Potato Stew)

Typically eaten during the summertime when fresh green beans are available at farmer's markets, this makes an excellent side dish for barbecued meats.

½ cup olive oil

1 large onion, finely chopped

2 lbs (1 kg) fresh green beans, cut into 2-in (5-cm) pieces

6 medium potatoes (any kind), cut into eighths

1 cup crushed tomatoes (fresh or canned)

2 tsp sea salt

1 tsp freshly ground black pepper

7 small (approximately 6-in/15-cm long) zucchinis, cut into 1-in (2.5-cm) cubes

Heat olive oil in a large saucepan on medium. Add the onion and sauté until lightly browned, about 3 minutes. Stir in the green beans and cook for about 5 minutes, or until beans turn a bright green color. Add potatoes, tomatoes, salt, pepper, and enough water to cover and simmer for 15–20 minutes. Once the potatoes and green beans start to soften, add the zucchini.

Cover pot and simmer until sauce is thick, about 30-45 minutes. (If there's too much liquid, increase the heat, remove the lid, and boil until juices have reduced.)

Makes 4 servings.

BRIAM (Roasted Root Vegetables)

A staple in any Greek home, Briam is a lovely and hearty vegetarian meal. Serve as a main course with crusty bread, a chunk of feta cheese, and Kalamata olives, or as a side with roasted lamb (p. 89).

2 medium potatoes (Yukon gold preferred), sliced like thick fries
3 medium yams, cut in eighths
2 parsnips, cut in quarters
2 cups fresh green beans, tips cut off and sliced in half
1 cup fresh okra, tops cut off (optional)
1 long Japanese eggplant, cut into 1-in (2.5-cm) slices
1 medium onion, chopped
1 leek, sliced (white parts only)
2 garlic cloves, chopped
2 cups fresh tomatoes, finely chopped (or canned crushed tomatoes)
1 cup finely chopped fresh parsley
¾ cup olive oil
1 tsp sea salt (or to taste)
½ tsp freshly ground black pepper

Preheat oven to 375°F (190°C).

Combine all vegetables in a large baking pan. Add parsley and olive oil, and 1 cup water. Season with salt and pepper. Bake for approximately 1 hour, until vegetables are tender.

Makes 4–6 servings.

YIAYIA'S PSOMI (Grandma's Bread)

RYE BREAD

FOCACCIA BREAD

BREAD KOULOURIA (Sesame Rings)

Breads & Muffins

PITA BREAD

TURKISH PITA

HOMEMADE PIZZA

BUILD-YOUR-OWN MUFFINS

CLASSIC BRAN MUFFINS

YIAYIA'S PSOMI (Grandma's Bread)

When we were young, my mother baked bread each week. As we were coming home from school, we could smell the aroma of the baking from down the street, well before we walked into the house. What a wonderful way to welcome your family home—with freshly baked bread drizzled with extra virgin olive oil and sprinkled with sea salt.

4 tbsp regular or quick-rising yeast
2 qt/L buttermilk
2 eggs, lightly beaten
1 tbsp sea salt
¾ cup olive oil
8–10 cups all-purpose white flour
½–1 cup sesame seeds (optional)

Preheat oven to 400°F (200°C).

Start yeast as directed on package and allow to double in size (this will take 15–20 minutes).

Warm the buttermilk in a saucepan on low heat, but do not bring it to a boil. Remove from heat and pour into a large mixing bowl. Stir in the doubled yeast, then mix in eggs, salt, and olive oil to combine well.

Add flour a little at a time to buttermilk mixture until dough is soft and does not stick to your hands. Knead dough on a lightly floured surface for 5–8 minutes or until all flour has been incorporated and the dough is smooth (it shouldn't be either sticky or dry). Cover and let the dough rise for 30 minutes (the dough should be full of small air bubbles when ready).

Shape dough into 6 loaves. Place into oiled loaf pans (the loaves should come only halfway up the sides of the pans, at this point). Brush tops of the loaves with olive oil and sprinkle with sesame seeds if desired. Cover and let sit in a warm place until they have doubled in size (approximately 2 hours).

Place loaves in the oven and bake for 30–40 minutes or until lightly browned. Remove from oven, let cool, then tap the loaves out of bread pans and let cool completely on a rack.

You can also use this dough to make buns and/or breadsticks. For buns, bake for 20–25 minutes; breadsticks need only 15 minutes.

Makes 6 loaves.

RYE BREAD

My mother taught me how to make this bread. Rye bread is very dense and makes a filling sandwich. Try making one with thinly sliced mortadella sausage, marinated artichokes, grilled vegetables, and a little Dijon mustard. Delicious!

1 tbsp yeast
6 cups rye flour
6 cups white flour
2 tbsp sugar
2 tbsp olive oil
2 tsp sea salt

Preheat oven to 400°F (205°C).

Dissolve yeast in 2 cups warm water in a large mixing bowl. Beat in 4 cups of rye flour by hand or using a hand-held or stand mixer. Cover and let rise for 1–1½ hours. Uncover the dough and thoroughly mix in 2 cups of water, the white flour, sugar, olive oil, salt, and the remaining 2 cups of rye flour. Knead for 2–5 minutes, until the dough is smooth, but be sure not to overwork it. Let sit covered for 20 minutes.

Form dough into 4 loaves and place in oiled loaf pans. Cover and let rise in a warm place for 40 minutes, or until the loaves have risen by ⅓ of their size.

Bake for 40–60 minutes. Brush loaves lightly with water when you take them out from the oven to prevent them from getting too hard. Let cool, then tap out of bread pans, and let loaves cool completely on a rack.

Makes 4 loaves.

FOCACCIA BREAD

My daughter Evangeline is the baker of the family, following in the footsteps of my grandfather. Focaccia is great for making sandwiches or mini-pizzas. Whatever you do, use fresh herbs in the dough. The caramelized onions add a nice touch.

homemade pizza dough (see p. 171)
¼ cup finely chopped fresh sage
¼ cup fresh finely chopped rosemary
2 tbsp olive oil
sea salt, to taste

Caramelized onions: (optional)
¼ cup olive oil
1 medium onion, finely chopped

Preheat oven to 400°F (205°C).

Follow recipe for homemade pizza dough, but do not top or bake.

Once dough has risen, knead sage and rosemary into dough. Roll into 3 or 4 8-in (20-cm) round x 1-in (2.5-cm) thick loaves and place on a lightly oiled baking sheet. Brush tops with olive oil and sprinkle with sea salt.

Bake for 30 minutes. (Optional: Remove from oven after 15 minutes and top with caramelized onions, see below. Return to oven and bake for another 15 minutes.) Remove from oven and place on a cooling rack.

Caramelized onions:
Heat olive oil in a frying pan on medium. Add onions and sauté until browned (caramelized), about 15–20 minutes.

Makes 3–4 loaves.

BREAD KOULOURIA (Sesame Rings)

A traditional Greek pretzel-like bread, koulouria are eaten at breakfast with strong cheese (such as Kefalotiri) and olives.

2 cups all-purpose, unbleached white flour
½ tsp sea salt
½ tsp sugar
2 tbsp yeast
4 tbsp olive oil
1 egg, separated
about ½ cup sesame seeds

Preheat oven to 400°F (205°C).

Combine flour, salt, sugar, and yeast in a large mixing bowl. Stir in olive oil, ½ cup warm water, and egg yolk. Cover and let rise for 30 minutes. Once the dough has risen, knead well.

Form dough into ring shapes, about 1-in (2.5-cm) thick and 4-in (10-cm) round. Brush with egg white and sprinkle with sesame seeds.

Place on an oiled baking sheet and let rise for another 30 minutes. Bake for 25–30 minutes or until lightly browned.

Makes about 30 koulouria.

PITA BREAD

My daughters loved this bread as kids. We would make it for breakfast and top it off with crumbled feta or Kefalograviera, a hard Greek cheese, diced tomatoes, and fresh oregano. Of course, it can also be used to wrap up souvlaki (p. 86) or chickpea patties (p. 151) with fresh veggies drizzled with tzatziki sauce (p. 28).

1 tbsp quick-rising yeast
½ tsp sugar
1 tsp sea salt
6–8 cups unbleached white flour
¼ cup olive oil
1 tsp dried thyme (or oregano)
½ cup grated Kefalograviera cheese (or any hard, salty cheese)

Mix yeast with 2 cups warm water in a large bowl. Add sugar and let sit for 10 minutes, or until bubbles begin to form.

Combine the salt and flour in a large bowl. Stir in the bubbling yeast mix and olive oil and combine to form a soft dough. Cover and let rise for 30 minutes. Punch down dough and roll into 6 to 8 round, flat pieces, about ½-in (1-cm) thick.

Heat olive oil in a large frying pan and fry pitas for 2 to 4 minutes on each side, or until golden brown on the outside and cooked through in the center. Sprinkle with dried herbs and grated Kefalograviera cheese.

Makes 6–8 pitas.

TURKISH PITA

Just like my mother made! This pita tastes best with Kasseri cheese (a Greek cheese found at most Mediterranean delis), but can also be made with sharp Cheddar, mozzarella, or cheese of your choice. Great to dip with tzatziki (p. 28) or hummus (p. 26), or can be used to wrap souvlaki (p. 86) and chickpea patties (p. 151).

4–5 eggs
1 cup milk
½ cup olive oil
1 tbsp butter, melted (optional)
2 medium zucchinis, grated
sea salt, to taste
freshly ground black pepper, to taste
2 cups unbleached white flour
2 cups crumbled feta cheese
⅓ cup grated Kasseri cheese (optional)

Preheat oven to 350°F (180°C).

Beat eggs in a large mixing bowl. Add milk, olive oil, butter, zucchini, salt, and pepper. Add flour and mix well until a cake batter consistency is reached. Add feta (and Kasseri or alternate cheese, if using).

Pour batter into an oiled 9 x 12-in (23 x 30-in) baking pan and bake for 45 minutes or until golden brown.

Makes 4–6 servings.

HOMEMADE PIZZA

Using this recipe, you can make fantastic pizza dough (thick crust or thin—your choice) and top with fresh vegetables, cheeses, and/or grilled or smoked meats.

1 tbsp instant yeast
2 tsp sugar
pinch of sea salt
2 tbsp olive oil
5–7 cups all purpose, unbleached white flour

Preheat oven to 400°F (205°C).

Mix yeast and sugar with 2 cups warm water in large mixing bowl. Cover with a tea towel and let stand for 10 minutes, until yeast begins to bubble.

Stir in salt and olive oil. Add enough flour, a cup at a time, until dough is not sticky. Knead for 5–8 minutes, until dough is smooth. Cover bowl and let dough rise for 30 minutes.

Knead dough again and roll out to desired pizza-crust thickness, then place on a large and lightly oiled round or square pizza dish. Cover and let rise for another 30 minutes.

Top pizza dough with homemade tomato sauce (p. 96), grated cheeses, fresh sliced vegetables, and slices of salami, sausage, or other cured meats, as desired, and bake for 20-25 minutes if a thin crust, 30 minutes if thicker, or until crust is golden brown. (Color is a more reliable indicator of readiness than time for this crust!)

Makes 2 9–12-in (23–30-cm) pizzas, depending on crust thickness, about 3–4 servings.

BUILD-YOUR-OWN MUFFINS

A basic muffin recipe that you can tailor to your tastes. Add blueberries, raisins, apples, grated carrot, chopped walnuts, or zucchini and dark chocolate. Be creative! Also try cinnamon, nutmeg, and/or lemon or orange zest for extra flavor.

¾ cup olive oil

1 cup sugar

2 eggs

1½ tsp vanilla extract

2 cups all-purpose unbleached white flour (or a mix of white and whole wheat flour for a more dense muffin)

pinch of sea salt

3 tsp baking powder

1 cup milk

Optional:

1 cup blueberries

1 cup raisins or currents

1 cup grated carrots or zucchini

¾ cup chopped walnuts

¾ cup dark chocolate chips

Preheat oven to 375°F (190°C).

Combine olive oil and sugar in a large mixing bowl. Add eggs and vanilla extract and blend until smooth. Mix flour, salt, and baking powder (and any dry spices you may be using) in a separate mixing bowl. In alternating batches, add flour mixture and milk to egg mixture and blend well. (If using fruits, nuts, spices, or other flavorings, add them in now.)

Pour batter into 2 oiled 12-cup muffin trays and bake for 25 minutes or until tops of muffins are lightly browned and a toothpick inserted in the center comes out clean.

Makes 24 muffins.

CLASSIC BRAN MUFFIN

A classic muffin, here made even healthier with olive oil. When in season, add fresh berries.

4 cups unbleached, all-purpose
   white flour (or a mix of white and
   whole wheat flour
for a denser muffin)
1 cup rolled oats
¾ cup wheat bran
3 tsp baking powder
2 tsp baking soda
½ tsp sea salt
1 tbsp cinnamon
1 cup olive oil
¾ cup brown sugar
3 eggs
1½ cups buttermilk or milk
4 tbsp molasses
¾ cup raisins
½ cup walnuts (optional)

Optional (add one only):
3 mashed bananas
2 apples, peeled, cored, and diced
1 orange, peeled and diced
1 cup pineapple chunks (fresh or canned)
1 cup fresh blueberries or raspberries

Continued next page.

Preheat oven to 400°F (205°C).

Combine flour, oats, bran, baking powder, baking soda, salt, and cinnamon in a large mixing bowl.

In a separate bowl, mix together olive oil, brown sugar, eggs, buttermilk (or milk), and molasses and blend well. Add liquid ingredients to the dry, mixing until well-combined. Add raisins, nuts, and fruit of choice (if using).

Pour batter into 1½ oiled 12-cup muffin trays. Bake for 25–30 minutes, or until tops of muffins are lightly browned and a toothpick inserted in the center comes out clean.

Makes 18 large muffins.

APPLE CAKE

THREE-LAYERED CHOCOLATE CAKE

WALNUT CAKE WITH SYRUP

LOUKOUMADES (Greek Doughnuts)

ALMOND BISCOTTI

— Desserts —

MELOMAKAROUNA (Honey Cookies)

TAHINI KOULOURIA (Sesame Cookies)

BASIL ICE CREAM WITH CORINTHIAN
BALSAMIC CARAMEL

OLIVE OIL ICE CREAM WITH BRANDY COOKIES
& RED WINE FRUIT CARAMEL

APPLE CAKE

Never underestimate apples. This delicious cake is as simple as it gets, and my daughters adore it. Gala or Red Delicious are good choices for this recipe, but any kind of apple will work well. You can add 1 cup of fresh blueberries to the batter when in season.

¾ cup olive oil
1 cup sugar
1 cup milk
1½ tsp vanilla extract
1 egg
1½ cups unbleached
   all-purpose white flour
3 tsp baking powder
1 tsp sea salt

Topping:
1 tbsp sugar
1 tsp cinnamon
4 apples, peeled and cored

Preheat oven to 350°F (180°C).

Combine olive oil, sugar, milk, vanilla extract, and egg in a large mixing bowl. Beat (using a hand-held or stand mixer) at medium speed until creamy. Slowly add all dry ingredients and continue to mix well.

Pour batter into a well-oiled 9-in (23-cm) round or square cake pan.

Cut apples in half and, using paring knife, gently score the top of each apple. Arrange the apples on top of cake and press them into the batter. Mix sugar and cinnamon together in a bowl. Sprinkle mixture on top of batter.

Bake until a toothpick inserted in the center comes out clean, about 45–60 minutes. Let cool before serving.

Makes 4–6 servings.

THREE-LAYERED CHOCOLATE CAKE

Chef Rob Cordonier, Hillside Cellars Winery, Naramata, BC

A decadent three-layer chocolate-lover's dream. Moist and delicious, this cake will have your guests pleading for more! Serve with Basil Ice Cream with Corinthian Balsamic Caramel, p. 185.

Cake:
3 eggs
¾ cup sugar
½ cup whole milk
¼ cup all-purpose flour
¾ cup + 2½ tbsp almond flour
  (almond meal)
2½ tbsp cocoa powder
5½ tsp baking powder
¾ cup extra virgin olive oil
½ tsp ground cinnamon

Chocolate Icing:
2 cups dark chocolate chips
¾ cup liquid whipping cream
1 vanilla bean
1 cup whipped cream

Preheat oven to 325°F (160°C).

Lightly brush an 8 in (20 cm) straight-sided cake pan with melted butter. Line the bottom of the pan with a circle of parchment cut to fit exactly in place.

In the bowl of an electric mixer fitted with a whisk, whip the eggs and sugar together on high until the mix is pale and has more than doubled in volume. Reduce mixer speed to medium and slowly add the milk.

Sift together the flour, almond flour, cocoa powder, and baking powder in a bowl. Add the dry ingredients to the egg mixture and gently incorporate on low speed. Add the olive oil in a slow stream with the mixer still on low. Lastly, add the cinnamon and mix until just incorporated.

Continued next page.

Pour the batter into the prepared cake pan and bake approximately 20 minutes, until a toothpick inserted into the center comes out clean. Allow to cool completely.

To prepare the icing:
Place chocolate chips in a stainless steel mixing bowl.

Heat the whipping cream in a double boiler. Add a split and scraped vanilla bean. Bring to a simmer, then pour over the chocolate and let sit for 2 minutes. Whisk the chocolate until smooth. Strain out the vanilla solids, then allow the mix to cool to room temperature.

Gently fold the already whipped cream into the chocolate mix in 3 equal batches.

To assemble the cake:
Even off any slight peak that may have formed on top of the cake so that it is level. Slice cake into 3 equal layers. Place one slice of the cake on a flat plate. Evenly spread approximately ¼-in (6-mm) of icing over the top of the bottom layer (a cake ring lined with plastic is useful during this process but not essential).

Spread ¼-in of icing evenly over the top of the second layer. Place the third layer of cake on top and gently press to even out the icing.

Repeat this process with the second layer. Remove the cake rings, if using, then ice the top and sides of the cake.

Slice with a hot knife into desired serving sizes.

Makes 1 cake (8–12 servings).

WALNUT CAKE WITH SYRUP

*A delectable cake. Serve warm, with a generous dash of syrup over top,
for rave reviews.*

8 eggs, separated
1 cup sugar
1 cup olive oil
1½ cups fresh orange juice
1 tsp orange zest
2½ cups flour
1 tsp baking powder
1 cup walnuts, finely chopped

Syrup:
2 cups water
1 cup sugar
1 cinnamon stick
1 tbsp lemon juice
½ cup brandy (optional)

about 2 tbsp icing sugar

Preheat oven to 375°F (190°C).

Beat egg whites until fluffy with a hand-held or stand mixer. Add sugar and continue mixing, adding 1 egg yolk at a time. While continuing to mix, slowly pour in the olive oil and orange juice, and mix in the orange zest.

Combine the flour and baking powder in a separate bowl, then add to the liquid mixture. Stir in the walnuts.

Pour batter into an oiled 9-in (23-cm) round cake pan and bake for about 45 minutes or until a toothpick inserted in the center of the cake comes out clean. When cake has cooled slightly (but is still warm), remove from baking pan and place on a serving dish.

To make syrup:
While cake is baking, combine all ingredients in a small saucepan and bring to a boil. Let boil until sugar has completely dissolved, then reduce heat to low and simmer for 30 minutes. Remove from heat and let cool to room temperature. Pour syrup over cake while the cake is still warm. Sprinkle top with icing sugar.

Makes 1 cake (8–12 servings).

LOUKOUMADES (Greek Doughnuts)

Loukoumades are a Greek-style doughnut ball drenched in sweet honey and topped with toasted sesame seeds. Simply addictive—and great served with a cup of strong coffee.

1 tbsp instant or regular yeast
1 tsp sugar
8 cups unbleached all-purpose white flour
½ tsp sea salt
about 4 cups olive oil (for deep fryer)
1 tsp cinnamon
about ¼ cup sesame seeds, toasted
about ½ cup honey

Dissolve yeast and sugar in ½ cup warm water in a small bowl. Set aside until the yeast mixture has doubled in size, 15–20 minutes.

Add flour, salt, and enough water to knead into a loose dough. Cover and let rise for about 4 hours.

Heat olive oil in a deep fryer to 375°F (190°C). Form pinches of dough into 1-in (2.5-cm) balls. Drop into hot olive oil and fry until golden brown, about 2–3 minutes—being very careful not to get splattered with the hot oil!

Remove the loukoumades and place on a paper towel to drain. Sprinkle with cinnamon and sesame seeds, and drizzle with honey. Serve warm.

Makes about 35–50 doughnut balls.

ALMOND BISCOTTI

I love to make biscotti, especially during the holidays. These are great any time of year, warm from the oven and served with a cup of coffee for dunking.

5¼ cups unbleached all-purpose white flour
6 tsp baking powder
2¼ cups whole almonds, unblanched
6 eggs
2 cups sugar
1 cup olive oil
6 tsp vanilla extract
2 tsp almond extract
3 tsp orange zest
1 egg white

Preheat oven to 350°F (180°C).

Combine the flour, baking powder, and almonds in a large mixing bowl.

In another bowl, beat together the eggs, sugar, olive oil, vanilla and almond extracts, and orange zest.

Add the wet ingredients to the dry and mix well until a soft, slightly sticky dough is formed. If dough is too sticky, add a little more flour; it shouldn't stick to the cutting board.

Place dough onto a floured cutting board and knead into a smooth ball. Cut dough into 6 equal pieces. Roll each piece into a 12-in (30-cm) long log about 3 in (8 cm) in diameter. Place logs on an unoiled cookie sheet, 3 in (7.5 cm) apart.

Beat the egg white in a small bowl until fluffy, then use to brush tops of the biscotti logs. Bake for 20 minutes. Remove from oven and let cool for 5 minutes.

Place logs onto a cutting board and cut diagonally into ¾-in (2-cm) thick slices. Stand the biscotti upright on the cookie sheet and bake for another 25 minutes, or until golden brown. Remove from oven and let cool on a rack. Store in an airtight container for up to six months or freeze for up to a year.

Makes 48 biscotti.

MELOMAKAROUNA (Honey Cookies)

Melomakarouna are traditionally prepared during the Christmas holiday season. In Greek folklore, the honey-laden sweets were meant as bribes for St Nick to bring the best gifts and St Vasilis to bless all with a prosperous new year. The full flavor of the walnuts and the sweetness of the honey make these cookies hard to resist at any time of the year.

2 cups olive oil
1 lb (½ kg) unsalted butter
1 cup sugar
1 cup fresh orange juice
9 cups flour (approx.)
3 tbsp baking powder
1½ tbsp cinnamon

Syrup:
2 cups honey
2 cups sugar
2 cinnamon sticks

1 cup finely chopped walnuts

Preheat oven to 350°F (180°C).

Heat olive oil and butter in a small saucepan on medium. When butter has melted, remove from heat and let cool to room temperature.

Blend sugar, orange juice, and the butter and oil mixture in a food processor. Slowly add in flour, baking powder, and cinnamon until the dough is smooth, soft, and malleable (it shouldn't be too stiff or sticky).

Pinch off 1 tbsp of dough to form oval-shaped cookies.

Place cookies on an unoiled cookie sheet and bake for 25 minutes or until lightly browned. Remove from oven and let cool.

To make syrup:
Combine all ingredients with 2 cups of water in a saucepan and bring to a boil. Reduce heat to medium-low and simmer for 15 minutes. Remove from heat.

While the syrup is still warm, dunk each cookie into it for about 20 seconds. (The cookies should be moist but not soggy.)

Place each cookie in a paper muffin cup, to catch the syrup. Sprinkle with chopped walnuts and arrange on a platter.

Makes approximately 90 cookies.

TAHINI KOULOURIA (Sesame Cookies)

Tahini is a paste made from ground sesame seeds available at most health food stores or Mediterranean delis. Dip these traditional cookies into a cup of strong coffee and enjoy!

2 cups sugar
2 cups olive oil
1 cup tahini
1 tsp vanilla extract
1 tsp orange zest
6 cups flour
2 tsp baking powder
½ tsp baking soda
1 tsp cinnamon
1 cup freshly squeezed orange juice
1 cup sesame seeds

Preheat oven to 350°F (180°C).

Blend sugar and olive oil in a food processor, then add the tahini, vanilla, and orange zest, and blend until creamy.

Combine the flour, baking powder and soda, and cinnamon in a separate bowl. Slowly add to the tahini mixture, alternating with the orange juice, until the dough has reached a soft but not sticky consistency.

Roll dough into 6-in (15-cm) long pieces, approximately ½-in (1-cm) thick. Bend each piece in half without breaking the long piece in two (so it looks like two legs side by side). Take one of the "legs" and cross it on top of the bottom one. (It should look like a folded ribbon).

Place cookies on a lightly oiled cookie sheet and sprinkle with sesame seeds. Bake for 15–20 minutes, or until the cookies are lightly browned.

Makes 36–48 cookies.

BASIL ICE CREAM WITH CORINTHIAN BALSAMIC CARAMEL

Chef Rob Cordonier, Hillside Cellars Winery, Naramata, BC

Olive oil ice cream with fresh herbs? Your eyes aren't tricking you. Whether sweet or savory, olive oil does it all. You'll need an ice cream maker to prepare this.

2 cups half-and-half
¼ cup finely chopped fresh basil
1 tbsp finely chopped fresh mint
¼ cup finely chopped fresh Italian parsley
2 cups cream
½ vanilla bean
½ cup sugar
6 egg yolks
1 baguette, cut into 16½-in (1-cm) square slices (croutons)
Curly leaf parsley sprigs, for garnish

Blend together the herbs with the half-and-half in a blender. Stir together the herbed milk, cream, vanilla bean, and ¼ cup sugar in a heavy bottomed pot on high and scald.

Whisk the yolks into the remaining sugar and temper in the scalded cream by adding a couple of tbsp of cream to the egg before adding back into the cream. Reduce heat to medium while constantly stirring for 4–5 minutes, or the mixture is of a consistency to coat the back of a spoon.

Strain herbs out of the mixture and let cool completely. (For best results, refrigerate mixture overnight.) After it has cooled completely, place the mixture into the ice cream maker, and according to the ice cream maker's instructions.

Continued next page.

Corinthian Balsamic Caramel:
7 tbsp heavy cream
1 ¼ cups sugar
2 tbsp glucose
¼ tsp sea salt
⅔ cup Corinthian balsamic reduction*
3½ tbsp olive oil

Warm cream in a small saucepan on low heat (do not boil) and set aside. Combine ¼ cup of water with sugar, glucose, and salt in a heavy bottomed pan on high. Bring to a boil to dissolve sugar, then reduce heat to medium and cook until mix is a dark golden caramel.

Pour the warm cream over the caramel and whisk to combine well. Remove the pan from the heat and whisk in the balsamic reduction, then whisk in the olive oil. Serve ice cream scoops drizzled with the balsamic caramel sauce.

*Corinthian balsamic reduction is made by simmering 3 cups of balsamic vinegar until it reduces to ⅔ cup.

Makes about 1½ qt/L ice cream.

OLIVE OIL ICE CREAM WITH BRANDY COOKIES IN RED WINE FRUIT CARAMEL

Chef David Beston, Jericho Tennis Club, Vancouver, BC

In the south of France, where olives are a predominant part of both the landscape and the cuisine, olive oil ice cream is common. I picked up the original idea and formula from Edouard Loubet of Le Moulin de Lourmarin restaurant in Provence, and have been playing with it ever since. Here is its current incarnation, served with fruits in a rich red wine and brown butter caramel. (You'll need an ice cream maker to prepare this.)

Olive Oil Ice Cream:
5 egg yolks
⅔ cup sugar
2 cups milk
7 tbsp olive oil
2 cups sour cream (or crème frâiche)

Over a hot water bath in a double boiler, whip the egg yolks, sugar, and milk until stiff. Fold in olive oil and sour cream. Freeze and process in an ice cream maker according to its instructions until set.

Crispy Brandy Cookies:
(Note: you'll need an empty, clean egg carton to form the cookies)
¼ cup butter
⅜ cup packed brown sugar
2 tbsp + 2 tsp corn syrup
2 tsp lemon juice
zest of 1 lemon
2 tsp brandy
½ cup all purpose white flour
pinch ground ginger

Continued next page.

Preheat oven to 350°F (180°C).

Melt butter and brown sugar in a large saucepan on medium, then stir in all the wet ingredients. Sift in the dry ingredients and mix until it forms a thick dough.

Scoop 2-tbsp balls onto an oiled baking sheet or silicone sheet. Bake for about 8 minutes and remove from oven.

While cookies are still warm, work quickly to gently press each one into an empty slot in the egg carton to form a slight bowl shape—the better to hold the ice cream.

Makes 12–15 cookies.

Red Wine Fruit Caramel:
½ cup unsalted butter
½ cup sugar
3 cups red wine
12 dried black figs
12 fresh strawberries

Melt butter and sugar in a saucepan on medium. Cook until the sugar caramelizes. The odor of browned butter (reminiscent of hazelnut) should fill the saucepan (the French call this brown butter noisette). Deglaze the saucepan with red wine, and reduce the sauce over high heat. After 5–7 minutes, add the figs.

After about 10 minutes, add the strawberries for a final minute of reduction. When the caramel develops a coating consistency, remove from heat. (Depending on the speed of the reduction, this could take 8–12 minutes.)

To assemble:
Divide the fruit and caramel sauce evenly into 4 or 6 bowls (depending on the portion size you wish to serve). Place a brandy cookie on top of each mound of fruit, being careful to ensure that it is secure.

Place a scoop of olive oil ice cream inside each of the cookies. If desired, sprinkle a chiffonade of lemon balm leaves over each dish. Serve immediately.

Makes 4–6 servings.

INDEX

Note: Recipe titles are in **bold**.

GUEST CHEFS' BIOGRAPHIES

LISA AHIER studied at the Culinary Institute of America, where she graduated with honors before training with Melissa Kelly at the Old Chatham Sheepherding Company in New York. While working with Kelly, she developed the passion for organic food and local sourcing that has since defined her career. Ahier has earned a variety of accolades, including Top Tables from *Gourmet* magazine. After moving to Canada, she and her husband Artie opened the highly acclaimed SoBo restaurant in Tofino, BC. Her work has been profiled in *Saveur, Food & Wine*, and the *New York Times. enRoute* named SoBo one of Canada's Best New Restaurants (2003).

DAVID BESTON began working in restaurants when he was fourteen years old and finished his culinary apprenticeship at the Chateau Whistler in 1999. While traveling abroad, he was guided and inspired by Edouard Loubet's two-Michelin-starred restaurant, Le Moulin de Lourmarin in France, as well as by Jerry Traunfeld, former Chef at the Herbfarm in Washington State. Beston says: "I learned the importance of how food is grown. The best chefs are also producers, and are in contact with the top growers." Beston was Sous-Chef at the Vancouver Club, taught at the Art Institute of Vancouver, and has been Executive Chef at Vancouver's Jericho Tennis Club since 2007.

After graduating from George Brown College in Toronto, **ROBERT CLARK** spent ten years training in some of Toronto's finest kitchens and apprenticing and working under some of Canada's "top toques." In 1992, Clark helped open Star Anise in Vancouver to critical acclaim. It remains the only restaurant to win the *Vancouver Magazine* awards for "Restaurant of the Year" and "Best New Restaurant" in the same year. Clark has been Executive Chef of Vancouver's C Restaurant since 1998; C's distinctive cuisine and wine lists have garnered innumerable awards from critics across the continent, and Clark has been repeatedly recognized for his outstanding dedication to working with sustainably harvested seafoods.

ROBERT CORDONIER completed his basic culinary education at the University College of the Cariboo and apprenticed at the Fairmont Chateau Whistler Resort under Executive Chef Vincent Stufano. Not long after, as a senior member of the culinary brigade at the Four Seasons Resort Whistler, Cordonier aided the successful opening of the award- winning Fifty Two 80 Bistro. In Vancouver, Cordonier served as Restaurant Chef at Herons Restaurant, at the Fairmont Waterfront Hotel. Cordonier is now at Hillside Cellars Winery in Naramata, BC.

"At an early age," says **CHRISTOPHE KWIAT-KOWSKY**, "I knew that food was my calling." He took the culinary program at Institut de Tourisme et d'Hôtellerie du Quebec. Upon completing the program, he combined it with another passion—travel. At seventeen, Kwiatkowsky moved to France and apprenticed in a one-star Michelin restaurant. He continued to learn, cook, and eat his way through England, Germany, and the West Indies before settling in Vancouver in 1990 to cook aboard one of the Cunard Cruise Line ships. He owned and operated a restaurant in Nelson, BC, for two years before joining the Fairmont Hotel Vancouver as a Sous Chef for five years. "It was there I discovered my love of sharing knowledge and skills with others in my profession." Kwiatkowsky became a culinary instructor before opening the Northwest Culinary Academy of Vancouver in 2004.

LYNDA LAROUCHE was formerly Executive Chef of Watermark Restaurant in Vancouver, BC. She acquired her Red Seal from Vancouver Community College after an apprenticeship with Cordon Bleu Chef Lucien Collette. In 1980 Larouche joined the Teahouse restaurant, later becoming Executive Chef at sister restaurant Seasons in the Park in 2003. Larouche's recipes have been published extensively in cookbooks and magazines. She has developed recipes for Oxford Landing wines of Australia and has been asked to develop a recipe for Campbell's Soup. She hopes to publish her own cookbook some day. One of Lynda's favorite memories is cooking for Bob Hope. He was in BC on a fishing trip and arrived at the Teahouse with his own crab. Talk about catch of the day!

TONY MINICHIELLO graduated with a Drama/Theatre degree from McGill University, but the "intense food culture" of the Mediterranean, he says, influenced his decision to enroll at the Institut de Tourisme et d'Hôtellerie du Quebec in Montreal. For the next four years, he cooked in French and Italian fine dining restaurants, large hotels, and catering kitchens in various cities. He co-owned a successful café and catering operation in the early 1990s, and spent the next seven years developing his skills as a chef instructor for four years at Dubrulle (Art Institute of Vancouver). Minichiello opened the Northwest Culinary Academy of Vancouver five years ago, and has been attracting a wide profile of students.

FRANK PABST has held tenure in Michelin-starred restaurants throughout Germany and France, including La Bécasse (Aachen), the Hôtel Negresco (Cannes), and Restaurant de Bacon (Antibes), where he was trained in rigorous classical cooking techniques. Pabst has directed the kitchens at Blue WaterCafe since 2003, serving fresh, sustainable seafood —Blue Water Cafe is a founding member of the Vancouver Aquarium's Ocean Wise program— and winning praise for his trademark "complexity without complication." His awards include Vancouver Magazine Chef of the Year in 2010, a silver medal in the 2009 Canadian Culinary Championships, Vancouver Culinary Champion of 2008 from Gold Medal Plates, and 2008 Chef of the Year from the Georgia Straight Golden Plate Awards.

JEAN-FRANCIS QUAGLIA comes naturally to the culinary world; his mother is acclaimed Chef Suzanne Quaglia of Marseilles' famed Le Patalain. At the age of sixteen, he enrolled at the École Hôteliere de Marseilles. Quaglia worked briefly at Le Patalain, and later at Le Chateau de la Chevre d'Or (Relais & Chateaux). At the two-Michelin-starred Hôtel Negresco in Nice, Quaglia met a young Canadian, Alessandra Mossa, who later became his wife. In 1992, Quaglia began his Canadian career as Sous-Chef under Bruno Born at award-winning Le Coq D'or restaurant in Vancouver. In 1994, Born took Quaglia with him to be Chef de Cuisine at the newly opened Sheraton Wall Centre's Azure seafood restaurant. The Quaglias opened their own restaurant, Provence Mediterranean Grill in 1997, and in 2002 opened a second location, Provence Marinaside. Their cookbook *New World Provence* (Arsenal Pulp) was published in 2007.

LIANA ROBBERECHT began her training with the Professional Cooking Program at Northern Alberta Institute of Technology and passed the Red Seal qualifying examinations in 1995. In 1998 she completed the Dubrulle French Culinary School Professional Pastry Arts and Desserts Program. As Executive Chef at the Calgary Petroleum Club since 2002, Robberecht is passionately committed to regional cuisine. A farm-to-table philosophy pervades the three kitchens and staff of forty-five under her leadership. This commitment extends out from her kitchen to include fellow chefs, diners, and food enthusiasts in the community at large as evidenced by her involvement in professional organizations and participation in special and educational events for the public.

Born and raised in Quebec, **RONALD ST. PIERRE** discovered his passion for cooking while in high school. He trained at Institut de Tourisme et d'Hôtellerie du Quebec and after graduation accepted a position at the internationally acclaimed resort Les Trois Tillieuls (Relaix & Chateaux). After leaving Quebec in 1982, St. Pierre worked in Vancouver in some of the city's most distinguished hotels, then moved to Vancouver Island in 1991 where he worked at the Old House Restaurant. Now, as chef and owner of LOCALS in the Comox Valley, he is committed to raising his guests' awareness about local foods and sustainability.

After working his way though some of the finest kitchens in Canada, **VINCENT STUFANO** became Executive Chef of the Fairmont Chateau Whistler in November 1997. He studied culinary arts at the British Columbia Institute of Technology (BCIT) and developed his career at Vancouver restaurants and hotels such as Chez Daniel, La Belle Auberge, and the Pan Pacific Hotel, as well as the Oak Bay Beach Hotel in Victoria. Stufano was appointed Executive Sous-Chef of the Fairmont Chateau Whistler in 2003. His culinary philosophy reflects the growing trend toward a healthier, down-to-earth lifestyle. Working with neighboring farmers to seek out the finest in regional, local organic produce is the essence of his cuisine.

JAMES WALT is Whistler's only chef to cook at the celebrated James Beard House in New York City. In 2000, he moved to Vancouver to open Blue Water Cafe. He served as executive chef to the Canadian Embassy in Rome, an experience that has shaped the way he cooks today. "The European market culture has inspired me to cook even more locally and seasonally," he says. Now living in the heart of Pemberton, BC's farming community, Walt serves the freshest local ingredients as *Araxi's* executive chef. His cookbook—*Araxi: Seasonal Recipes from the Celebrated Whistler Restaurant*—has won multiple international awards, as well as a nomination from New York's James Beard Awards.

ABOUT THE AUTHORS

Helen Koutalianos was a food columnist and Greek cooking instructor who now runs Basil Olive Oil Products Ltd. with her husband Basil. The company imports extra virgin olive oil from a grove in Greece that Basil's family has owned for four generations.

Anastasia Koutalianos is Helen Koutalianos' daughter; she has worked in editing, book and magazine publishing, and historical research. A lifelong foodie who learned everything she knows about cooking from her mother, she is also a promotions and event planner (*nadatodo.com*).